D1130200

the art of solitude

yale

university

press

new haven

and

london

stephen

batchelor

the art of

solitude

a meditation on

being alone with

others in this world

Published with assistance from the foundation established in memory of Philip Hamilton McMillan of the Class of 1894, Yale College.

Copyright © 2020 by Stephen Batchelor. All rights reserved. This book may not be reproduced, in whole or in part, including illustrations, in any form (beyond that copying permitted by Sections 107 and 108 of the U.S. Copyright Law and except by reviewers for the public press), without written permission from the publishers.

Yale University Press books may be purchased in quantity for educational, business, or promotional use. For information, please e-mail sales.press@yale.edu (U.S. office) or sales@yaleup.co.uk (U.K. office).

Set in Adobe Garamond type by IDS Infotech, Ltd.
Printed in the United States of America.

Library of Congress Control Number: 2019943488
ISBN 978-0-300-25093-0 (hardcover : alk. paper)

A catalogue record for this book is available from the British Library.

This paper meets the requirements of ANSI/NISO Z39.48-1992 (Permanence of Paper).

10 9 8 7 6 5 4 3 2 1

Retreat into yourself, but first of all make yourself ready to receive yourself there. If you do not know how to govern yourself, it would be madness to entrust yourself to yourself. There are ways of failing in solitude as in society.

—MICHEL DE MONTAIGNE

For oft when on my couch I lie
In vacant or in pensive mood,
They flash upon that inward eye
Which is the bliss of solitude;
And then my heart with pleasure fills,
And dances with the daffodils.

—WILLIAM WORDSWORTH

contents

preamble

Solitude is a fluid concept, ranging from the depths of loneliness to the saint's mystic rapture. In his poem *La Fin de Satan* the novelist Victor Hugo declared that "the entirety of hell is contained in one word: *solitude*." He later conceded: "Solitude is good for great minds but bad for small ones. It troubles brains that it does not illuminate." Yet Hugo was unable to go as far as his older English contemporary William Wordsworth, for whom solitude was a "bliss" that filled the heart with joy. Largely avoiding its extremes of hell and bliss, here I will explore the middle ground of solitude, which I consider a site of autonomy, wonder, contemplation, imagination, inspiration, and care.

I will treat solitude as a practice, a way of life—as understood by the Buddha and Montaigne alike—rather than seeking to analyze it as a discrete psychological state. I recognize isolation and alienation as the dark, tragic sides of solitude. Woven into our mortal condition, they are equally part of what it means to be alone, whether in a monastic cell, an artist's studio, or a troubled marriage. Solitude, like love, is too complex and primal a dimension of human life ever to be captured in a single definition. I don't intend to "explain" solitude. I seek to disclose its extent and depth by telling stories of its practitioners.

This book is a multifaceted, paratactic exploration of what has supported my own practice of solitude over the past forty years. Spending time in remote places, appreciating and making art, practicing meditation and participating in retreats, drinking peyote and ayahuasca, and training myself to keep an open, questioning mind have all contributed to my ability to be alone and at ease with myself.

In 2013, I turned sixty. I took a sabbatical from my work as a teacher of meditation and philosophy, and spent much of the year traveling, studying, and making collages. In January I went by bus from Mumbai to Bhopal to visit the ancient rock-cut temples of India; in March, I attended a colloquium at the Barre Center for Buddhist Studies in Massachusetts on the emerging field of Secular Buddhism; in October I made a pilgrimage to South Korea to honor the thirtieth anniversary of the death of my Zen teacher Kusan Sunim; and in November I flew to Mexico to participate in a medicine circle with Don Toño, a shaman of the Huichol tribe.

At the Barre colloquium, the dharma teacher and scholar Gil Fronsdal presented his work on an early Buddhist scripture in the Pali language called the *Chapter of Eights* (*Aṭṭhakavagga*). In their directness, simplicity, and austerity, the 209 verses of the *Chapter of Eights* capture the pithy utterances of the Buddha as he "wandered alone like a rhinoceros" in the years before he established a community. Largely devoid of Buddhist terminology, the verses advocate a life liberated from opinions and dogmatism.

The *Chapter of Eights* made a deep impression on me. Intrigued by the possibility that the four eight-verse poems near the beginning of the text might be the earliest record of the Buddha's teaching, I decided to translate them into English. Inspired by their rhythm and metaphors, I treated them as poetry rather than scripture. I titled my translation the *Four Eights*.

The *Four Eights* opens by raising the question of solitude itself:

> The creature concealed inside its cell—
> a man sunk in dark passions
> is a long, long way from solitude.
> FOUR EIGHTS, I:I

I translated the Pali term *guhā* as "cell," though it could have been rendered as "cave" or "hiding place." *Guhā* is also linked to the word *guyha*, which means "secret." We can hide away and feel safe within the dark, silent interior of a cave. We can likewise retreat to those intimate places within ourselves that seem to afford comparable protection, where we can pursue our secret lives, alone and undisturbed.

In a letter to her friend Monna Alessa dei Saracini, the fourteenth-century scholar and mystic Catherine of Siena wrote:

> Make two homes for thyself, my daughter. One actual home in thy cell, that thou go not running about into many places, unless for necessity, or for obedience to the prioress, or for charity's sake; and another spiritual home, which thou art to carry with thee always— the cell of true self-knowledge, where thou shalt find within thyself knowledge of the goodness of God.

The "creature concealed inside its cell" need not be a nun meditating in a convent. It could be anyone who feels herself isolated and lonely in a bustling, noisy city. Yet either of these solitary people, remaining consumed and paralyzed by private anxieties, would, for the author of the *Four Eights*, be "a long, long way from solitude."

There is more to solitude than just being alone. True solitude is a way of being that needs to be cultivated. You cannot switch it on or off at will. Solitude is an art. Mental training is needed to refine and stabilize it. When you practice solitude, you dedicate yourself to the care of the soul.

For those who have rejected religion in favor of secular humanism, the notion of solitude may imply self-indulgence, navel-gazing, or solipsism. Inevitably, some may be drawn to solitude as a way of escaping responsibility and avoiding relationships. But for many it provides the time and space to develop the inner calm and autonomy needed to engage effectively and creatively with the world. Moments of quiet contemplation, whether before a work of art or while observing your breath, allow you to rethink what your life is about and reflect on what matters most for you. Solitude is not a luxury for the leisured few. It is an inescapable dimension of being human. Whether we are devout believers or devout atheists, in solitude we confront and explore the same existential questions.

My accounts in this book of ingesting psychedelics in shamanic ceremonies should not be taken as a blanket endorsement of their use. I am describing a journey rooted in my own personal and cultural history that may or may not be pertinent to the reader.

Most Buddhists, moreover, would regard taking peyote and aya-huasca as an infraction of the moral precept against intoxicants and thus incompatible with the practice of the dharma. A princi-pal motive in writing *The Art of Solitude* has been to try to find a more constructive way of talking about the contentious issue of drugs in our highly medicated society. As the current opioid epi-demic in the United States illustrates, both secular and religious institutions struggle to find ways to respond intelligently and compassionately to this crisis. Rather than basing a response on the binary opposition between indulgence (bad) and absti-nence (good), we need a more informed and nuanced under-standing of how to use substances that modify human awareness, feeling, and behavior. By framing the use of psychedelics within the practice of solitude, I seek to integrate it into a broader cul-tural discourse that includes meditation, therapy, philosophy, reli-gion, and art.

This book grew out of my wanderings, explorations, and stud-ies but was shaped by my twenty-year practice of making collages from found materials. Wherever I go, I collect discarded scraps of paper, cloth, and plastic, which I glue onto card stock, then cut up and organize into square mosaics. This process transforms random bits of rubbish into artworks structured by formal rules decided on in advance, making each collage a combination of chance and order. *The Art of Solitude* has been conceived and ex-ecuted in a similar way. While writing I have borne in mind the strict metric structure of the *Four Eights* as well as the chaotic or-ganization of Montaigne's *Essays*, both of which have inspired the form of this book.

Montaigne observed that in painting "sometimes the work breaks free from the painter's hand, surpassing his ideas and understanding, leading him to be astonished and profoundly moved." The grace and beauty of such works is achieved "not only without the artist's intention but without his knowledge." Likewise, "a good reader often finds in others' writings gems other than those placed there or even noticed by the author, endowing those texts with richer meaning and character." In composing this book as a collage, I have sought to reduce my authorial control, thereby freeing the text to find a voice of its own.

My collages are exercises in composition and differentiation. As this process has evolved, I have become absorbed by the question of *how different things go together*. One of my guiding principles is that of noncontiguity. This means that no two pieces I cut from the same material can be adjacent to each other in the final composition, thus ensuring that each piece of the collage is maximally differentiated from the pieces around it. This enables every piece to stand out vividly in its own "solitude" from the matrix of which it is also an integral part. I have employed the same principle to write this book. None of its thirty-two chapters is ever preceded or followed by a chapter that treats the same theme. And since the sequence of chapters is partly decided by random selection, this meant that I had no idea when writing a particular chapter what other chapter would precede or follow it in the final work. Each chapter, therefore, had to be written as a piece that would be able to stand alone. By abandoning any logical or narrative continuity between successive chapters, I allow the disparate themes and topics of the book to bounce off one another in surprising and illuminating ways.

This project has returned me to my own beginnings as a writer. My first book, published in 1983, was called *Alone with Others: An Existential Approach to Buddhism.* As I put it then, I was intrigued by the paradox of "always finding ourselves inescapably *alone* and at the same time inescapably *together with others.*" I recognize now that a comparable aesthetic tension has informed my collage work. Drawing upon Western phenomenology and existentialism, *Alone with Others* presented a Buddhist understanding of human fulfillment ("awakening") as the integration of wisdom (*alone*) and compassion (*with others*). My interest in solitude is still driven by the same desire to make sense of this basic paradox of human existence.

While this book recounts—sometimes explicitly, sometimes implicitly—the inner story of my own struggle with Buddhism, and while I continue to draw on sources and themes from that tradition, I do not consider *The Art of Solitude* to be a Buddhist book. I am not interested in presenting a Buddhist interpretation of solitude. I want to share with you what practitioners of solitude, from varied backgrounds, disciplines, and traditions, have reported back from the coalface of their practice.

For the Chinese, to turn sixty means to have completed five twelve-year cycles of the zodiac. Each additional year of life is regarded as a bonus, a gift. In Korea, the strict behavioral conventions of Confucian society are relaxed at sixty. You often encounter groups of seniors tramping through the hills, singing songs, drinking *soju,* and making fools of themselves. I consider the five-year period it has taken me to write this book as a gift. I hope I have not squandered it.

My translation of the *Four Eights* is included as an appendix. All material originally in French, Pali, and Tibetan has been newly translated for this book by the author.

Stephen Batchelor
Aquitaine, France
JUNE 2019

the art of solitude

I

Even on long summer days in rural England when it would not get dark until 10 PM, my mother insisted on sending her two sons to bed early, which I thought both unfair and pointless. Unable to sleep, I would close my eyes and imagine my prone body in its pajamas moving up and down the walls of the bedroom, gliding against the ceiling, then remaining stationary at a point of my choosing. I had no doubt that I was actually in those impossible locations rather than lying on my bed. I performed these maneuvers night after night. I took them very seriously. I never spoke to anyone else about what I was doing. They were exercises in pure solitude.

Another contemplation during those sleepless evenings was to dwell single-mindedly on a taste that was not of this world. This taste was neither pleasant nor unpleasant, only entirely different from all other tastes I knew. It was deeply familiar though I had no idea where it came from. Now I can just about summon up a distant, ever receding hint of its flavor.

I had recurrent dreams of flying. With minimal effort I would soar through the air, swooping and climbing as I wished. The landscapes below me were bathed in sunlight, vividly detailed and rich in color. As the dreamer I was aware that these dreams were more real than other dreams. As soon as a flying dream began, my dreaming self would rejoice. Awake again, I would recall these flights with the nostalgia of one who has been cast into a leaden realm.

Sometimes I would try as hard as I could to bring my thinking to a stop. My constant failure to do this troubled me. I was powerless in the face of the implacable flood of thoughts pouring forth. Or I would pick my way back through the waking day in a quest to find moments when I was free of worries. When I thought of myself as "happy," I was aware of a pale shadow of anxiety hovering nearby. Something could always go wrong.

These were my first naïve, unguided attempts at what I would now call meditation. Exploring the textures and contours of my interiority enabled me to escape the boredom and loneliness of a sleepless child and discover the contented self-sufficiency of solitude. Thomas De Quincey talked of "that inner world, that world of secret self-consciousness, in which each of us lives a second life apart and within himself alone, collateral with his other life, which he lives in common with others." At school it puzzled me why none of the teachers acknowledged, let alone addressed, the presence of this inner life. Only when I met Buddhist monks did I first encounter people who were at home in this realm and talked about it openly, without embarrassment or reserve.

2

Embrace what you perceive and cross the flood.

The sage is untied to possessions—

having extracted the arrow, take care—

Don't long for this world or the next.

FOUR EIGHTS, 1:8

In 1570, at the age of thirty-seven, Michel de Montaigne sold his counselorship in the Parliament of Bordeaux, a post he had held for thirteen years, in order to devote himself to a life of solitude. He converted a three-story fortified tower on his manorial estate into a retreat. The ground floor served as a chapel, the middle floor as his living quarters, and the top floor as the library. The attic space above the library housed the estate bell. "Every day, at daybreak

5

and sundown," he wrote, "a great big bell sounds the Ave Maria. This racket makes my very tower shake."

On one wall, Montaigne inscribed his intention: "to withdraw and lie my head on the bosom of the Wise Virgins, where, in calm and serenity, I will pass the rest of my days." Relieved of the pressures of public service, he would devote himself to liberty, tranquility, and leisure. This was easier said than done. "The greatest service I could do for my mind," he had thought, "would be to leave it in complete idleness to care for itself, bring itself to a stop, and settle down." Instead,

> like a runaway horse galloping all over the place, it gave birth to weird, fantastic monsters, one after another, without order or design.

Unable to cope with this turmoil, he fell into depression. He lifted himself out by conducting a close observation and analysis of his inner life, which he wrote down in the hope of "making my mind ashamed of itself." So began his career as a philosopher and essayist.

Turmoil was not confined just to his mind. It raged all around him. Eight years earlier, in 1562, a bloody civil conflict between Catholics and Protestants erupted throughout France. The province of Guyenne, where he lived, was a major center of these religious wars, which would rage intermittently for the rest of his life. In the first year of violence, the nearby church of Montcaret was destroyed by Catholic troops in the battle to recover it from Protestants. The church of Saint-Michel-de-Montaigne, only a five-minute walk from his home, was burned to the ground. "The place where I dwell," he writes, "is always the first and last to be bombarded by our troubles." He recounts that he has frequently gone to bed imagining that he would be "betrayed and bludgeoned to death that very night."

During Montaigne's first summer in his tower, King Charles IX and his mother, Catherine de Medici, triggered the St. Bartholomew's Day Massacre. Fearing an uprising to avenge the attempted murder of the Protestant Admiral de Coligny, they ordered the assassination of all leading Protestants in Paris. Mob violence erupted, and Catholics rampaged through the streets attacking Protestants. The carnage spread through twelve other cities in France, including Bordeaux. Around ten thousand Protestants were slaughtered.

Montaigne admitted that when younger he could have been tempted to "share in the risks and challenges" of the Reformation. Inspired by figures like the Christian humanist Erasmus, he embraced the resurgence of reason and classical philosophy that characterized the Renaissance. His closest friend, Étienne de la Boétie, was the author of *Voluntary Servitude,* a discourse on the tyrannical nature of governments. At the request of his father, Montaigne had translated *Natural Theology,* a Latin work of the fifteenth-century Catalan doctor and philosopher Raimond Sebond. Sebond argued for an understanding of God inferred from observations of the natural world, thereby reconciling the demands of faith and reason, religion and science.

A year after the outbreak of civil war, Étienne de la Boétie died of dysentery at the age of thirty-two. Montaigne was devastated. His love for Étienne was an intellectual and emotional cornerstone of his life. He describes their friendship as one where "souls are blended and merged with each other in so perfect a union that the seam which joins them is effaced and can no longer be found." La Boétie bequeathed his books to Montaigne, and they became the core of the library in the tower. He remained forever, I imagine, the implied reader of the *Essays*.

To honor the memory of his friend, Montaigne intended to include *Voluntary Servitude* in the first volume of his essays. He abandoned this idea on discovering that it had already been published "to an evil end by those who seek to upset and change the state of our political system without caring whether it will be an improvement." A similar fate befell his translation of Raimond Sebond's *Natural Theology,* which had also found favor among Protestant thinkers. This resulted in Montaigne's longest essay, a book-length mea culpa entitled *An Apology for Raimond Sebond,* in which he rejects Sebond's belief in the redemptive power of reason and replaces it with a philosophy of radical ignorance and unconditional faith.

For ten years he studied, thought, and wrote in his tower. The first edition of the *Essays,* in two volumes, was published in 1580 in Bordeaux. Montaigne was forty-seven. As befitted a loyal *seigneur,* he immediately left for Paris to present a copy to the new king, Henry III. Having made a favorable impression at court, he set off on a journey that took him through Switzerland, Germany, Austria, and much of Italy. He arrived in Rome at the end of November.

Montaigne went to Rome in order to make himself available to replace the outgoing French ambassador to the court of Pope Gregory XIII. As a gentleman of the Chamber of the King of France, a devout Catholic, a scholar fluent in Latin, and now a philosopher and man of letters, he was well suited for this position. Since he was also a gentleman of the Chamber of the young Protestant King Henry of Navarre (who was also governor of Guyenne and second in line to the French throne), Montaigne would be an invaluable negotiator between the two sides in the wars of religion. He rented spacious lodgings, visited the historical sites, had an audience with the pope, and submitted the *Essays* to the papal authorities for approval. Then he waited patiently for the letter from Paris that would decide his fate.

"Ambition," he had written in his essay "On Solitude," included in the book now under scrutiny in the Apostolic Palace, "is the humor most at odds with retreat. Fame and repose cannot share the same lodgings." He criticized the Roman statesmen Pliny and Cicero for treating solitude as a judicious career move, a way to impress others with their learning and philosophical refinement. Those gentlemen, he observed, "just have their arms and legs outside society: their souls and thoughts remain more engaged with it than ever. They have stepped back only in order to make a better leap." Worldly renown, he declared, "is far removed from my calculations."

3

Three months after becoming a monk, I took off into the Himalayan foothills behind Dharamsala. I was twenty-one years old. My backpack contained a sleeping bag, groundsheet, towel, kettle, bowl, mug, two books, some apples, dried food, and a five-liter container of water. Monsoon had just ended: the sky was crystalline, the air cleansed, the foliage luxuriant. After three or four hours, I left the well-trodden footpath and followed animal trails up the steep, sparsely forested slope until I reached the grassy ledge hidden by boulders and sheltered by branches that I had identified on an earlier foray.

Inspired by stories of Indian and Tibetan hermits, I wanted to know what it was like to be cut off from all human contact, alone and unprotected. I would stay here as long as my meager supply of food and water permitted. No one knew where I was. If I fell and broke a leg, was bitten by a cobra or mauled by a bear, it was unlikely I would be found. High in this aerie,

I could still hear the distant horn blasts and grinding gears of buses and trucks below, which I regarded as an affront.

I would wake with my sleeping bag covered in dew. After peeing and meditating, I would light a fire, boil water, make tea, then mix it with roasted barley flour and milk powder to form a lump of dough. This was breakfast and lunch—following the monastic rule, I did not eat in the evening.

My meditations included the *sādhanā*s into which I had been initiated, where I visualized myself either as the furious bull-headed, priapic Yamāntaka or the naked, menstruating red goddess Vajrayoginī. I alternated these tantric practices with an hour of mindfully "sweeping" my body from head to foot, noticing with precision the transient sensations and feelings that suffused it. When not eating or meditating, I intoned a translation of Śāntideva's *Compendium of Training,* an eighth-century Sanskrit anthology of Mahāyāna Buddhist discourses, which I had vowed to recite in its entirety while up here.

"There never was a Buddha aforetime," declared the text in its Victorian English, "nor shall be in the future, nor is there now, who could attain that highest wisdom whilst he remained in the household life. Renouncing kingship like a snot of phlegm, one should live in the woodland in love with solitude. . . . As the herbs and bushes, the plants and trees fear not nor are afraid or terrified, so the Bodhisattva dwelling in the forest must regard his body as like to the herbs and bushes, plants and trees, like wood, like plaster on a wall, like an apparition . . ."

The *Compendium of Training* provides instructions on its own use. Once settled in the forest, the monk should "recite what he has read before thrice in the night and thrice in the day in a tone not too high and not too low, not with senses agitated, not with wandering thought, in all tranquility, putting away indolence." Without inhibition I let these words ring out into the silence of the ravines and the wind.

I still have my copy of this faded brown hardback. By the smudged purple stamp of the Piccadilly Book Stall, I assume I bought it in Delhi in the early 1970s. It lies open before me now. The musty, peppery smell I associate with Indian books of that time invades my nostrils. I am returned to the forest, to my red-robed younger self cross-legged on the ground, earnestly reciting Śāntideva's words in a place "overshadowed with trees, with flowers, fruit, and leaves, with no danger from rabid dogs, where caves are and mountain slopes, easy to traverse, peaceful, incomparable."

What remains of that solitude now is my memory of the sweeping panorama of the plains of the Punjab, the immense arc of the heavens, and the embrace of the mountains that harbored this fragile dot of self-awareness. Once, a fabulous multicolored bird launched itself from the cliffs beneath, floated for an instant in the air, then disappeared from view. A herdsman and his goats came close to discovering me one afternoon. I peeked at them through a lattice of leaves as the animals grazed and the wiry, sun-blackened man in a coarse wool tunic lay on a rock.

Supplies exhausted and text recited, I trekked back to my room in the village of McLeod-ganj below. During my five days on the mountain I had acquired a taste for solitude that has been with me ever since.

4

Nacho, his son Nacho, and I climb into a Mitsubishi Pajero, leave the grounds of the villa, and drive up into the wooded hills that encircle the old Indian town of Tepoztlán. I have eaten hardly anything all day and feel light-headed. Along the way we pick up the *mara'akame,* Don Toño, and his apprentices: Andrés, José-Luis, and Raúl. We stop at a farmhouse in the village of San Juan to collect a *metate,* a rectangular slab of what looks like dark pumice stone. The animated conversation suggests this is an object of some importance, but I cannot imagine why.

By the time we turn onto a steep dirt track in the forest, it is night. The SUV skids and whines as its wheels spin in the mud and leaves. We pile out and try to push it up the hill but to no avail. So we unload blankets, ponchos, bulging shopping bags, and the metate, divide them among us, and trudge ahead, guided by the unsteady beam of a flashlight. We can see our breath in the damp air.

We come to a clearing where a simple, crudely built structure stands. A circle of wooden pillars supports a pointed roof made of corrugated iron sheets. Apart from a low wall running around its edge, the space is open to the elements. In the middle of the pounded mud floor is a pit filled with ash and bits of charcoal. We put down what we are carrying, then head outside to gather firewood for the ceremony.

No one seems to be in a hurry. The others chat, joke, and smoke cigarettes. It takes an hour or so to carry and drag enough branches and logs into the circular space to start making the fire. The mara'akame spreads out a blanket, sits down, and begins unpacking the shopping bags. Feathered instruments appear around him, then a tasseled hat, hand drums, boxes of cheap candles, cups, and, finally, a package carefully wrapped in white cloth.

From the contents of another bag, Andrés has constructed a makeshift altar. Before a cheap print of the Madonna of Guadeloupe he sets out candles and oranges. He invites each of us to place the texts we had been asked to prepare on the altar. That morning, I had copied out by hand the third poem of the *Four Eights*. "The priest without borders," says its final verse,

> doesn't seize on what he's known or beheld.
> Not passionate, not dispassionate,
> he doesn't posit anything as ultimate.
> FOUR EIGHTS, 3:8

I hope to remain true to this sentiment. With as much reverence as I can muster, I place the folded sheet of paper before the Madonna.

Don Toño gestures for us to come over to him. He is a short, stocky, dark-skinned man, like many of the peasant farmers I have seen elsewhere in Mexico. Under the yellowish light of a paraffin lamp he unknots the cloth-wrapped package to reveal a half dozen fresh peyote cacti that he and Andrés collected from the desert the day before. Each plump, dull green *lophophora williamsii* is about ten centimeters in diameter, composed of six symmetrical segments. The mara'akame cuts them open and passes the pieces around. He shows me, the newcomer, how to extract the fibers that are embedded in the cactus's flesh. This fiddly operation done, each piece is crushed with a cylindrical stone on the metate, at the base of which a funneled ledge allows the juices to run off into a bowl.

The juice is diluted with water, then unceremoniously poured into disposable plastic cups. We each take one. Following the others, I sip this drink until the cup is empty, then scoop out with my fingers the remaining filaments of flesh. It has a slightly bitter but not unpleasant taste. I feel the cold liquid settle in my empty stomach.

The mara'akame asks me about my reasons for taking part in this gathering. I tell him I have turned sixty this year and want to take stock of my life, to step back and consider what I have accomplished over the past forty years as a student, practitioner, and teacher of Buddhism. To do this, I have decided to revisit my experience with psychedelics, which had a formative effect on me as a young man in turning me toward the dharma. Now I am interested in taking these substances in the context of a religious ceremony, under the guidance of a shaman, in the company of others, rather than simply swallowing a pill by myself or with friends.

We gather in a circle around the fire. The fierce, crackling blaze does not yet generate much heat. I sit cross-legged, covered by a red poncho of tightly woven coarse wool. Some distance away, the mara'akame lies down on the ground, pulls an electric blue blanket over himself, and goes to sleep. Nacho the younger begins beating out a simple rhythm on a drum.

For the first hour or two—I have no watch and little sense of the passage of time—I am convinced that nothing is happening. I feel a mild indigestion, which causes occasional burps of air that taste of mashed cactus. True, I experience a certain stillness and clarity, but no more than if I had spent the same amount of time meditating, which is what I have been doing. As I look around, no one else seems troubled. They talk in low voices, wander about to stretch their legs, tap on a drum for a while. I put my worries down to my inexperience with this new medicine.

5

on solitude

michel de montaigne

selected passages from the essays

It was a melancholic humor, and thus a humor much at odds with my nature, produced by the chagrin of the solitude into which I cast myself some years ago, that first put into my head this daydream to get involved in writing.

Now I believe that the sole end of solitude is for one to live more at leisure and at ease by oneself.

I am not by nature averse to the bustle of courts: I have spent part of my life in them and am used to cheerfully going about my business in such crowds—provided only occasionally and when it suits me. My fastidiousness, however, forcibly binds me to solitude. At home, in a busy household with many visitors, I see plenty of people but rarely those with whom I love to talk.

In ridding ourselves of the courthouse and marketplace we do not rid ourselves of the principal worries of our life. Ambition, covetousness, indecisiveness, fear, and desires hardly abandon us just because we change address. They pursue us into the monasteries and schools of philosophy themselves. Neither deserts nor caves nor hair shirts nor penance can extricate us from them.

That is why it is not enough to remove oneself from people, not enough to go somewhere else. We have to remove ourselves from the habits of the populace that are within us. We have to isolate our own self and return it to our possession. We carry our chains with us; we are not entirely free. We keep returning our gaze to the things we have left behind; we fantasize about them constantly.

Our malady grips us in the soul, and the soul cannot flee itself. So we must bring and draw it back into itself. That is true solitude: it can be enjoyed in towns and royal courts, but more conveniently apart.

The solitude which I love and advocate is primarily about bringing my emotions and thoughts back to myself, restricting and restraining not my footsteps but my desires and my anxiety, refusing to worry about external things, and fleeing for dear life from servitude and obligations: retreating not so much from the crowd of humanity but from the crowd of human affairs.

The philosopher Antisthenes joked that a man ought to provide himself with possessions that float, so they can escape the sinking ship with him.

Of course we should have wives, children, possessions, and, above all, health: but not to become attached to them in such a way that our happiness depends on them.

Let these things be ours, but not so glued and joined to us that we cannot detach ourselves from them without ripping off our own skin in the process. The greatest thing in the world is to know how to be for yourself.

We should set aside a room at the back of the shop, just for ourselves, quite isolated, where, as the principal retreat for our solitude, we establish our true freedom. In there we should resume our usual conversation with ourselves—in privacy, with no contact or communication with anything outside—where we can chatter and laugh to ourselves as though we had no wife, no children, no possessions, no attendants, and no valets. So that when the time comes to lose these things, it will be nothing new for us to be without them.

We have a soul that can turn in on itself; it can keep itself company. It has the means to attack and defend, to give and receive. Don't worry that solitude will find you hunched up in boredom.

We must do like those animals who erase their tracks at the entrance of their lairs. It should no longer be your concern that the world speaks of you; your sole concern should be with how you speak to yourself.

Retreat into yourself, but first of all make yourself ready to receive yourself there. If you do not know how to govern yourself, it would be madness to entrust yourself to yourself. There are ways of failing in solitude as in society.

When I dance, I dance; when I sleep, I sleep. When I am walking alone in a beautiful orchard, at times my thoughts are occupied by what's happening elsewhere, at other times I bring them back to the walk, to the orchard, to the sweetness of that solitude, and to myself.

To tell the truth, confined solitude broadens my horizons and expands me outward: I throw myself into the affairs of state and into the wide world more willingly when I am alone.

6

Without noticing how or when, I find myself in an altered state of mind. My awareness is subtly but acutely heightened. Ecstatic, I feel electric ripples course through my body, making me want to stretch and moan. My spine straightens, as though to optimize the contemplation that is taking hold of me. I no longer have to concentrate; it happens by itself. Distraction is not an option; all random thoughts have ceased. I am intensely, silently conscious as I gaze into the breathing orange heart of the fire.

Andrés gently shakes the mara'akame awake. Don Toño sits up, puts on the wide-brimmed hat whose tassels swing in front of his eyes, picks up a hand drum, and begins to intone a haunting chant to the rhythm of its beat. There is a hypnotic beauty and poignancy to whatever he sings in his nasal voice. Something ancient and mournful resonates through his words in the Huichol tongue. Andrés lights a cigarette and places it between Don Toño's lips. The mara'akame draws on it deeply and keeps drumming. Then he lies down again and goes back to sleep. This ritual is to be repeated several times during the course of the night.

Nacho the younger whispers in my ear: "What is the name of your grandfather?" I say: "Alfred." He says: "The fire is your grandfather. The Madonna is your grandmother." I sense that this is a cue for me to do something. I do not know what he means and feel no need to ask further. Immersed in my solitude, I am beatifically detached from everyone else while acutely aware of their presence and how it sustains me.

Raúl, a young workingman with dense black stubble, rises to his feet. He braces himself, spits into the fire several times, glares intently at the blaze, and launches into an impassioned confession. He wraps his arms around his body, rocks about unsteadily, wails and weeps as a torrent of words pours forth. At one point he makes as though to vomit into the flames, but without success. Andrés comes over and brushes Raúl's body from head to foot with feathers tied to a short stick that he then shakes at the fire as though dispelling droplets of water from them.

I am unmoved by but not dissociated from this unexpected demonstration of emotion. I feel utterly transparent and pure inside, yet entirely at one with Raúl's confession.

"Go talk to your grandfather," urges Nacho the younger. I ignore him.

A chipped enamel mug appears on the embers at the edge of the fire. We take it in turns to sip a hot brown beverage that warms and soothes the stomach. The taste is familiar but strange.

I learn that it is chocolate blended with dried peyote. Whether or not this additional dose has any effect I cannot tell. Such questions no longer hold any interest. All that matters is the undiluted intensity of the moment, the keen lucidity of the senses, the ecstatic silence.

There is drumming, more coordinated now, accompanied by dance. Andrés takes off his shirt, writhes and twists beside the fire, the sweat-dampened skin of his lean torso shining in the flames. He sits down beside me. In a mixture of English and French I ask him: "If peyote is the medicine, then what is the sickness it cures?" He says: "A closed heart."

By the time we are back in Tepoztlán later that morning, the night around the fire has assumed a dreamlike quality. A heightened lucidity and stillness of mind remain with me. The world continues to appear luminous and bright. I feel as if my senses, nervous system, and brain cells have been washed clean. It will be several weeks before the effect of the medicine fades away.

Did the mescaline in the peyote alone produce this? Would I have had the same experience had I taken exactly the same dose alone in my living room listening to Bach? Did the past forty years of practicing the dharma make a difference? I suspect that the crushing of the cacti, Grandfather Fire, the chants, the confessions, offering a poem to the Madonna, sitting cross-legged in meditation, the silence I observed, fasting the day before, my motives for participating in the ceremony all played a part.

I slowly come to understand that the ceremony served as an existential affirmation of what I had done and was doing with my life. For a few hours, in the language of Carlos Castaneda, it had "stopped the world" and allowed me to "see." In Buddhist terms, it had let me "behold" the "stopping of reactivity" and dwell in the "deathless." Without any need to be formulated in concepts or words, it confirmed that the life I had chosen as a writer, artist, and teacher was an appropriate one. I realized that were I to die, I would leave this world with no regrets.

Eighteen months later, I receive an email from Nacho the elder. "During a meditation session two days ago," he begins, "I realized for the first time how beautiful silence is. And I must say I learned a lot from you in this issue, especially when we were at Tepoztlán and you began to keep silent, more and more, it was even uncomfortable, until we almost all remained in silence and I understood." During all this time I had taken Andrés's comment about "a closed heart" to be a mild rebuke for my having failed to participate more actively in the ceremony. Now I am not so sure.

7

The maid sits at a dining table, head propped on her right arm. She is asleep. A plate of fruits, a closed decanter, and a fallen wineglass lie on the tablecloth before her. Through a half-open door I can see into another room behind. Whoever was here not long before has departed, leaving the girl alone with her reveries and dreams. If a lover has just stormed out, knocking over his glass, her face shows only weariness.

Johannes Vermeer kept returning to scenes of domestic solitude. A milkmaid stands in a kitchen pouring milk from an earthenware jug into an earthenware bowl on a table, her eyes and body in exact alignment for the trickle of white liquid to find its destination. She is serenely composed in the fulfillment of an everyday task. Like her, I too know what it is like both to pour milk from a jug and be conscious of pouring milk from a jug.

Around this time Johannes also painted a street scene in Delft, the city where he was born, lived, and died. He would have been in his late twenties, married with a steadily growing family. A woman sits in a doorway embroidering: two children kneel on the ground with their backs to the viewer—they might be spinning a top or playing with a kitten—and in an alley, a servant woman bends forward toward a broom. These human moments are nearly lost amid the chipped red brickwork, the cloudy sky, and the cobbled street. Absorbed in their tasks, these people inhabit their private worlds, oblivious to one another.

A woman sits behind a table, tuning a lute. Her eyes are turned toward a window, but her attention is elsewhere. I observe her listening to a sound only she can hear. A woman stands by a table where a silver water pitcher sits on a tray. With her left hand she holds the pitcher's handle; with her right she opens a window. She hovers in mid-movement, poised to be dazzled by the sun. A woman in a blue smock grips a letter in both hands. A pale light reveals her devouring eyes and parted lips as she digests the meaning of the words.

Vermeer captures from the inside what it is like to be human. He shows how it is for each of these women to be in silent, innocent conversation with herself. The Romanian philosopher Emil Cioran called Vermeer the "master of intimacy and confidential silences," who "softens the impact of solitude in an atmosphere of familiar interiors." These women are not nuns or hermits. They are briefly at rest in a world of bourgeois comfort and domestic routines. They are alone but do not appear lonely.

Between the forefinger and thumb of her right hand a woman suspends a delicate pair of scales over a table. The fingers of her left hand rest on the tabletop. Two open boxes, a yellow ribbon, pearl necklaces, and gold coins are spread out on its surface. Her gaze rests on the empty scales. She smiles faintly. Her muted features are bathed in a radiance that cannot be accounted for by the feeble sunlight from the curtained window. This secular Madonna appears indifferent to the riches before her.

The inner ease of these women is revealed as much by the paintings' compositional harmony, subdued colors, and play of light as by any facial expression or bodily posture. There is nothing static about this solitude. An almost photographic realism catches the figure as she slips between what has just happened and what is about to come. I glimpse a fleeting passage in a story I cannot know. There are no hard lines or contours in these works. Vermeer uses the technique of *sfumato:* the smoky blurring of edges, where one color (that of a sleeve) merges imperceptibly into another (that of a wall). This blurring heightens the illusion of depth and amplifies the poignant slippage of time.

A young woman in a yellow, ermine-trimmed jacket stands looking at herself in a mirror as she tries on a pearl necklace. I observe her observing herself. I sense her delight in herself. Another woman in the same jacket sits at a table writing a letter with a quill pen. She looks aside in midthought, searching for the right word or phrase. I see her thinking to herself. A girl bends over her worktable, immersed in sewing a piece of lace. I share her quiet joy in her craft. These women are self-sufficient in their solitude, each at ease with herself and her lot in life.

The citizens of the seventeenth-century Dutch Republic were prosperous enough to afford paintings that depicted the genteel leisure to which they aspired. The scenes of domestic contentment were also consoling diversions from an unstable and violent reality. In 1654, when Vermeer was twenty-one, thirty tons of gunpowder exploded in Delft, wrecking a quarter of the city, taking more than a hundred lives (including that of his fellow artist Carel Fabritius, painter of *The Goldfinch*), and injuring thousands. In the *rampjaar* of 1672, the Dutch found themselves simultaneously at war with France, England, and the prince-bishops of Münster and Cologne. As a defensive measure against invasion, they opened the dykes and flooded the low-lying land, which precipitated widespread economic collapse. Vermeer's widow, Catharina, recorded that thereafter her husband was unable to sell any work. He died suddenly three years later of unknown causes at the age of forty-three, leaving eleven daughters.

Apart from thirty-five surviving paintings and perfunctory mentions in parish, legal, and commercial records, we know nothing about Johannes Vermeer. Despite their naturalism, his works do not show what Vermeer saw either; they show what he, his patrons, or his clients wanted us to see. As I study them today in museums from Vienna to New York, I find myself looking for Vermeer. He must have stood, sat, or paced for many hours before these canvases stretched on their wooden supports. These objects from his world become fleetingly part of mine. He manufactured these things, fussed over them, struggled with them. As I peer at his solitary women, I see them seeing him. Their faces become the mirror in which he is reflected.

8

on mindfulness

gotama, the buddha

selected passages from the pali canon

If members of other traditions ask: "How did the wanderer Gotama mainly dwell during the three-month-rains retreat?" you should say: "During the rains, friends, he dwelt mainly in the collectedness that is mindfulness of breathing."

If one could completely say of anything: "That is a noble dwelling, that is a sacred dwelling, that is the dwelling of a true person," it is of collectedness that is mindfulness of breathing that one could say this.

The practitioner goes to a forest, to the root of a tree or to an empty hut. She sits down, crosses her legs, straightens her back, and establishes mindfulness at the opening of her mouth and nostrils. Mindfully she breathes in, mindfully she breathes out. Breathing in deep, she knows: "I breathe in a deep breath"; breathing out deep, she knows: "I breathe out a deep breath." Breathing in shallow, she knows: "I breathe in a shallow breath"; breathing out shallow, she knows: "I breathe out a shallow breath." She trains thus: "Feeling the entire body I will breathe in. Feeling the entire body I will breathe out." She trains thus: "I will breathe in calming my bodily inclinations. I will breathe out calming my bodily inclinations."

Just as when a skilled turner or his apprentice makes a long turn, he knows: "I make a long turn," and when making a short turn, he knows: "I make a short turn," so too, when the practitioner breathes in a deep breath she knows: "My breathing is deep," and when she breathes in a shallow breath, she knows: "My breathing is shallow."

In this way, she dwells contemplating the body as a body internally, externally, and both internally and externally. Or she dwells contemplating bodily phenomena as they arise, as they vanish, as they both arise and vanish. Or else the recollection "This is a body" is simply established in her to the extent necessary for bare knowledge and mindfulness.

When walking, she understands: "I am walking"; when standing, she understands: "I am standing"; when sitting, she understands: "I am sitting"; when lying down, she understands: "I am lying down"; or she understands accordingly however her body is disposed.

Again, she is one who acts in full awareness when going forward and returning; when looking ahead and looking away; when flexing and extending her limbs; when wearing her robes and carrying her bowl; when eating, drinking, and tasting; when shitting and pissing; when walking, standing, sitting, falling asleep, waking up, talking, and keeping silent.

In these ways, she dwells independent, not clinging to anything in the world. This is how one dwells contemplating the body as a body.

9

In order to manage their solitude, human beings in all cultures throughout history have medicated themselves. To this end they have sought out, prepared, refined, and ingested a wide range of substances from sugar to coffee, cigarettes to vodka, aspirin to heroin, cannabis to peyote. These medicines make you feel better in and about yourself. Instead of being overwhelmed by petty worries, you can tolerate and transcend them. When medicated, your levels of stress decline, your headaches go away, your anxiety disappears, boredom and loneliness vanish. You feel at ease in your aloneness, your senses are stimulated, you are more comfortable with others, and your imagination is often activated.

In his 1954 essay "The Doors of Perception," an account of taking mescaline for the first time, the English novelist and philosopher Aldous Huxley acknowledges that it "seems most unlikely that humanity at large will ever be able to dispense with Artificial Paradises."

> Most men and women lead lives at the worst so painful, at the best so monotonous, poor and limited that the urge to escape, the longing to transcend themselves if only for a few moments, is and has always been one of the principal appetites of the soul.

Despite these deep longings, modern societies have broadly adopted a fearful and repressive attitude to psychoactive substances. "For unrestricted use," observes Huxley, "the West has permitted only alcohol and tobacco. All other chemical Doors in the Wall are labeled Dope, and their unauthorized takers are Fiends." Today, with the legalization of marijuana in Uruguay, Canada, and ten American states, as well as a renewed wave of research into the therapeutic value of psychedelics, the tide may be slowly turning.

It cannot be denied that with many of these substances we run a considerable risk of becoming addicted to them. We easily get locked into a cycle of craving them, enjoying them, and feeling depressed when their effects wear off. We may become dependent on taking a substance simply to feel normal. In order to obtain it, we may sacrifice our health or resort to criminality to finance our addiction. The problem lies not only in the nature of the substances themselves but in our individual and social confusion as to how to use them. And at the root of this confusion lies the matter of how to care for our soul, govern ourselves, and manage our solitude.

The first cigarette I smoked as a young teenager in a shady patch of woodland made me dizzy and nauseous. I lay down in a sweat, my heart pounding, as I waited for its effects to pass. Such was the peer pressure around smoking tobacco and the allure that the culture of the time imparted to it that I managed to overcome my aversion to cigarettes. In truth, I could not quite see the point of tobacco. I never found it that pleasant, but for three or four years it became a habit nonetheless. I started drinking alcohol shortly afterward. At least beer and cider had the result of inducing euphoria and making me more socially at ease. But they also rendered me woozy, clumsy, and garrulous, and, if I drank too much, thick-headed, morose, and irritable for much of the next day. Again, none of these side effects dissuaded me from indulging in raucous, drink-fueled evenings with my friends.

Around the age of sixteen I was introduced to cannabis in the form of hashish. I found that it induced an enhanced state of awareness, which allowed me to consider my life with focused and lucid attention. When high on hashish, I marveled at the beauty of the natural world, enjoyed music and art more intensely, and became keenly aware of being a strange, self-conscious animal with thoughts, emotions, longings, and fears. Cannabis let me consider myself and the world from a perspective that was richer and more fascinating than that of ordinary consciousness. At times this could be troubling and even frightening, but the sharpened vision of life that it offered more than compensated for its dark side. It was through cannabis that I started becoming deeply curious about my own interiority and its possibilities.

During my final two years at school, I experimented with LSD. I must have taken it around twenty or thirty times. It produced a magnificently electrified version of what I experienced with cannabis. I was enraptured by the endlessly unfolding fractal patterns it produced behind my closed eyes; the sight of a beetle negotiating a blade of grass, the intricate webbing of a leaf, all raised to the level of mystical rapture. Even the one "bad trip" I had prompted a vision of Matthias Grünewald's sixteenth-century *Isenheim Altarpiece*—depicting the gruesome crucifixion and resplendent resurrection of Christ—and led me to hitchhike across France to see it, from Dinan in Brittany (where I had taken the LSD) to Colmar on the German border.

On becoming a monk at the age of twenty-one, I did not use any psychoactive substances for nearly ten years. Toward the end of my monastic training, while a monk in Korea, I occasionally smoked the leaves of the hemp plants the local farmers cultivated to make rope and cloth. After years of meditative training I found that I could better control the effects of cannabis. Instead of being spun off into trains of thrilling but incoherent thoughts, I could channel the power of the medicine to enhance my contemplation of the dharma. Not only could I reflect with greater acuity and precision, I was enabled to consider a topic from other angles altogether. In the sober light of hindsight, I would realize that some of the "insights" from such reveries were indeed fantastical, yet many turned out to be valuable advances in or confirmations of my understanding.

By taking cannabis as a monk, I learned that such substances generate a power in one's mind that is neither good nor bad in itself. What matters is whether or not you have the ability to turn this power to your own ends instead of being overwhelmed by it. In my case, this required that I first achieve a degree of self-governance through mastering a contemplative discipline rooted in a philosophical and ethical vision.

I also learned that such self-medication is as much about enhancement of performance as the elimination or reduction of painful feelings. I found that cannabis was best taken in solitude and silence while in a clear and untroubled state of mind. In terms of writing, I found that it helped envision the unfolding and development of a text and sharpen the ability to edit what had already been written. It was of little use, however, in the process of composition itself.

After I disrobed and came back to Europe as a married man, I developed a taste for wine. Though I would drink only in the evening as a way to relax and socialize, this turned into a daily ritual to which I became habituated. The routine was broken when I led or sat a meditation retreat but invariably resumed as soon as I returned home. I also continued to smoke cannabis by myself.

Contemporary liberal societies seem incapable of deciding on what constitutes acceptable substance use. Alcohol and tobacco are readily available, yet in 2016, in the United States alone, each day an average of 240 people died from alcohol-related causes and around 1,300 people from tobacco-related causes. Worldwide, the yearly death toll from consuming alcohol and tobacco is estimated to be about nine million. Despite these statistics, billions of dollars continue to be spent every year on advertising cigarettes, beer, wine, and spirits. By contrast, cannabis, peyote, and ayahuasca are criminalized, although people have taken them for centuries, often as religious sacraments, with seemingly minimal detriment to their physical or mental health.

Buddhism offers a simple solution: abstain. Advocating abstinence as the way to deal with substance abuse is like advocating celibacy as the way to deal with unwanted pregnancies and sexually transmitted disease. In theory, this is foolproof; in practice, it is completely unworkable. As long as we live in an open and tolerant society, people will continue to self-medicate just as they will keep on having sex.

Secular governments and traditional religions are losing the moral authority to legislate or offer guidance on these matters. For as long as modern societies condone the use of illegal substances by celebrated cultural figures, they weaken a commitment to the rule of law—particularly in the eyes of the young who treat these figures as role models. As long as religions refuse to endorse any approach except abstinence, they fail to provide an adequate and nuanced education concerning their use and misuse. And as long as we do not understand self-medication as one among other ways of managing our solitude, we lack the context in which to integrate it into disciplines of caring for the soul.

10

He lets go of one position without taking another—
he's not defined by what he knows.
Nor does he join a dissenting faction—
he assumes no view at all.

FOUR EIGHTS, 4:5

On writing down his ideas, Montaigne was surprised to discover that his natural disposition had a philosophical bent. He noted that a new character had been born: "the accidental philosopher." At the same time, he lamented that even for educated people of his day philosophy had come to mean something "speculative and vain, without use or value." He blamed this on an arid intellectualism ("thereforeism") that had turned the discipline into a grim, forbidding topic. For him there was nothing more "joyful, lively, or playful—I would almost say more sexy" than philosophy.

For Montaigne: "Astonishment is the foundation of all philosophy; inquiry the way it advances; and ignorance its goal." He recognizes and affirms "a kind of ignorance that is powerful and generous and no less honorable or courageous than knowledge." He calls such ignorance his "master form." It puzzles him that people are astonished only by "miracles and strange events" that seem to "hide themselves whenever I appear." By contrast, he declares:

> I have seen nothing more weird or miraculous than myself. Over time we get used to strange things, but the more I probe myself and know myself the more my oddity astonishes me and the less I understand who I am.

He quotes Socrates, "the wisest man ever," who, when asked what he knew, replied: "All I know is that I know nothing."

Strangeness is hardly restricted to oneself. "Just consider the fog through which we have to grope in order to comprehend the very things we hold in our hands," he suggests. "It is familiarity, rather than knowledge, that takes away their strangeness." Montaigne cites the Epicurean philosopher-poet Lucretius, who asks:

> Imagine if these things were shown to men now for the first time,
> Suddenly and with no warning. What could be declared
> More wondrous than these miracles no one before had dared
> Believe could even exist?

Montaigne was raised by his beloved but demanding father to be a Renaissance man. Until the age of seven, he was allowed to speak only Latin. His humanist education immersed him in the culture of ancient Greece and Rome. He came to live and breathe

the newly recovered works of Plato, Aristotle, Epicurus, Seneca, Plutarch, and others. He had favorite quotations painted on the beams and joists of his library for inspiration. He modeled himself on the eminent statesmen of antiquity, who ranged widely in their learning, not restricting themselves to one school of thought. He quotes Cicero: "I have to write, but in such a way as to affirm nothing; I shall always be seeking, mostly doubting, rarely trusting myself." Like Cicero, Montaigne kept circling back to the philosophical skepticism that originated with Socrates and Pyrrho.

Trained in the tradition of the "laughing" philosopher Democritus, Pyrrho accompanied Alexander the Great to India, where he studied with the sages encountered there. On returning to Greece, he led a simple life and taught philosophy. According to his student Timon:

> Pyrrho declared that things are equally in-different, un-measurable, and un-decidable. Therefore, neither our sensations nor our opinions tell us truths or falsehoods. We should not put the slightest trust in them, but be without judgment, without preference, and unwavering, saying about each thing that it no more is than is not, or both is and is not, or neither is or is not. The result for those who adopt this attitude will first be speechlessness, then untroubledness (*ataraxia*).

For Montaigne, "no other invention of the human mind has as much validity and utility" as Pyrrhonism, which presents man "naked, empty, and aware of his natural weakness." Pyrrhonists pursue an ongoing, open-ended inquiry that steers a middle way between affirmation and denial. Their aim, Montaigne says, "is to shake things up, to doubt, to inquire, to be certain of nothing, to vouch for nothing." He admits that this approach is difficult to grasp. "Whoever can imagine a perpetual confession of ignorance, an unbiased judgment in each and every situation, can conceive of Pyrrhonism."

For Montaigne, Pyrrhonists seek ataraxia in order to achieve "immobility of judgment." Montaigne defines ataraxia as

> a peaceful and settled way of life untroubled by the pressure of opinions and the knowledge we pretend to have of things, which give birth to fear, avarice, envy, immoderate desires, ambition, pride, superstition, love of novelty, rebellion, disobedience, and opinionatedness, as well as most of our bodily ills.

As freedom from opinion and passion, ataraxia is another word for the kind of solitude Montaigne seeks. To be truly alone requires that we settle in a still and clear state of mind no longer troubled either by obsessive thoughts or by conflicting emotions.

Philosophical skepticism, Montaigne says, "can best be conceived as a question: '*Que sçay-je?*'—'What do I know?' " This became his slogan. He had it inscribed on his emblem, which depicted a pair of scales, symbolizing a commitment not to favor one opinion over any other. Pyrrhonists call this balancing act "suspension of judgment" (*epoché*), a practice that extends from solitary reflection to conversations with friends. "I care little about what topics are being discussed," admits Montaigne. "All opinions about them are one to me; and I am more or less indifferent about which view emerges victorious."

"Pyrrhonist philosophers," according to Montaigne,

> cannot express their approach to life in any known way of speaking. They need a new language: for ours is entirely formed of affirmative

statements quite unacceptable to them. So when they say "I doubt," you can grab them by the throat and make them confess they know one thing for sure: that they doubt.

The essays are Montaigne's attempts at finding this new language. He continually expands them. They keep sprouting new shoots. He deletes or alters nothing except the occasional word. "I change subject arbitrarily and chaotically," he says. "My pen and mind roam about of their own accord. If you want less foolishness, you need a touch of madness."

No amount of probing the essays will ever capture who or what Montaigne *is*. That would be "like trying to seize hold of water in your fist: for the more tightly you squeeze something whose nature is to run everywhere, the more you lose what you want to hold on to."

II

I gaze out onto the patchwork of fields and scattered villages that melts into the blurred horizon of the Western Ghats. If I listen carefully, I can make out the faint rumble of traffic along the highway from Pune to Mumbai. Otherwise, it is as silent as it would have been for those who lived here in their rock-cut cells two thousand years ago. This silence is amplified by the hush of breeze that stirs the yellowed grasses of winter and sends flurries of tiny, chirping birds to flight.

I turn around to face Devil's Peak Monastery, carved by hand out of the dark basalt rock of the hillside that looms above me. To my left, accessible through a narrow defile, is the apsidal shrine room, about twelve meters deep, with a stone stupa at the end. To my right is the living area, also apsidal in shape, providing access, at regular intervals, to nine

Bedse, ground plan; based on a drawing by Dr. J Burgess, 1880

cells, each with two beds. The ground plan is based on a drawing by a Dr. J Burgess in 1880.

Apart from a forest-dwelling mendicant called Gobhūti and his disciple Asaḷamita, whose names are preserved in the sole inscription at the site, we have no idea who lived here. We do not know who painstakingly chipped out these spaces in the dense igneous rock with chisels of high tensile steel. Nor are there any inscriptions to tell us who supported them. The nearby rock-cut monastery at Kārla, however, records donations made by a group of benefactors including "the perfumer Siṃhadata, the carpenter Sāmi, the Greek Sihadhaya, the Greek Dhaṃma, and a certain Mitadevaṇaka."

Shaven-headed, ochre-robed mendicants sat cross-legged in these cells while Jesus spent forty days in the Judaean desert, fasting and being tempted by Satan. As far as we know, monks have not meditated here at Devil's Peak for eight hundred years, since

Buddhism disappeared from the Indian subcontinent. A herdsman from the local village of Bedse lies down in the sheltered shade of the living area, his face covered with a threadbare cloth, as his goats forage on the steep slopes.

Solitude has nothing to do with huddling inside a dark, cool cell high above the bustle of farm life below. Once the novelty wears off, you discover how seclusion magnifies the pressures and demands you feel. No matter where you hide your body, you cannot escape those timeworn habits of mind that keep reasserting themselves. For those like Gobhūti and Asāḷamita, who were no doubt familiar with the tricks and temptations of the Devil, the name of the monastery would have had a cruel, mocking edge to it.

I stand still in the shrine room. I am alone inside a sculpted void. The twenty-six pillars that run parallel to the walls serve no structural purpose. Remove them and nothing would happen. I forget that the pillars and stupa are simply the parts of the mountain that were not removed. They were already here before the chisels set to work to "reveal" them. Only the empty space in the hall has been created.

I cannot help but see the void in which I am standing as a metaphor for emptiness: the absence of compulsive reactivity, a precondition for the unimpeded space of paths that allow human flourishing. The unadorned simplicity of this rock-cut shrine evokes the Buddha's dharma before it mutated into dogma. This is nirvana inscribed in stone. Until the idea of emptiness was hijacked by metaphysicians, it was just another way of talking about solitude.

That "solitude" is a synonym for "nirvana" or "emptiness" is implied by the opening lines of the *Four Eights,* which read:

> The creature concealed inside its cell—
> a man sunk in dark passions
> is a long, long way from solitude.
> Hard is it to let go of what drives us,
>
> hard to be free from the wants
> that cleave to the thrill of being alive,
> hankering for what's gone and to come,
> hungering for those delights now—no one else can save you.
> FOUR EIGHTS, I:1–2

When I began to study these poems for their insights into solitude, I found myself equally fascinated by their "architecture." Each poem is composed of eight four-line verses, making up a total of thirty-two lines. The number of verses in the four poems is thus the same as the number of lines in each poem: thirty-two. The sequences, combinations, and symmetries of fours and eights exerted a powerful aesthetic attraction upon me. The poems appeared in my mind's eye as a square panel of thirty-two rectangles, four across and eight high: a grid waiting to be filled.

This metric verse structure also served as an aid to memorizing a work that was transmitted orally. Yet I refuse to accept such a utilitarian purpose as the sole explanation for composing the text in this way. The metered verses impose formal constraints on the author. For poets like the composer of the *Four Eights,* such constraints served as part of their discipline as artists. They faced a double challenge: to articulate an argument as lucidly and economically as possible while adhering to the formal design and cadences of the medium.

Like the rock-cut shrine at Devil's Peak, these poems are ruled by an aesthetics of emptiness. Each poem advocates and celebrates a life emptied of self-centered opinions. To realize such inner solitude, the poet has to get his own opinions and personality out of the way. Rather than tell us that opinions are confining and misleading, which is simply another opinion, he employs the structure of the poems to illustrate his point. I am reminded of W. H. Auden's eulogy:

> Blessed be all metrical rules that forbid automatic responses,
> force us to have second thoughts, free from the fetters of Self.

Adherence to the formal structure of the work constrains the poet's habitual impulses. He cannot just say the next brilliant thing that springs to mind. He has to find out what will and will not work within the limits of the form. This is not the dry rational calculation one might use to solve a technical problem. The verse form becomes an equivalent of the rock-cut cell: a confined space of solitude and contemplation that opens up the possibility of saying something that is not determined by familiar desires, fears, and aversions.

I leave the shrine room and walk across to the monks' living area. I enter the fourth narrow doorway on the left and sit cross-legged on one of the two rock beds inside the cell. The surface on which I am sitting is coarse and uneven, just as the walls and ceiling are. Running my fingers over the rock, I can feel the final indentations made by the chisel that formed the bed two thousand years ago. At the point where the bed joins the corner of the cell, I touch a small triangular patch of a smoother material. As my eyes become used to the pale light, I see that it is a surviving fragment of the plaster that once would have coated every surface in the tiny room.

12

I was introduced to the practice of mindfulness by S. N. Goenka in 1974, a few weeks after being ordained as a novice monk. Together with a group of young Tibetan monks and Western students of Buddhism, I attended a silent ten-day Vipassanā retreat in Dharamsala, India.

During the first three days we cultivated mindfulness of breathing by focusing on the sensation of the breath as it passes over the upper lip. After a while the fugitive passage of inhalations and exhalations consolidated into a stable point of sensation at the center of the lip. This point then became the exclusive focus of the meditation.

In becoming more concentrated, I started seeing flashes of colored lights and patterns in my mind. They did not last long, and we were advised to pay them no attention. By the end of the three days, I had settled into an unprecedented state of focused attention, which I could sustain for several minutes at a time without distraction.

On day four, we moved our focus from the upper lip to a point at the top of the head. From there we carefully expanded our attention to the rest of the scalp, the face, the ears, the neck, until we reached the torso. Then we slowly continued through the rest of the body, along each arm and leg in turn, until we reached the tips of our toes. Once this downward scan was complete, we repeated the procedure in reverse until we returned to the top of the head. We spent each meditation session "sweeping" the body from head to foot and back again.

At first, my experience was patchy. Some parts of the body buzzed, tingled, vibrated, and pulsed, while other parts felt almost completely insensate. As I persisted with the exercise—it was all we did for several hours each day—the dead zones began to come alive until I felt my entire body as one single mass of quivering sensations.

In a deep, reassuring voice, Mr. Goenka instructed us to pay attention to the range of pleasant, unpleasant, and neutral feelings associated with these sensations. A pain in the knee breaks down into physical reactions triggered by the stress on the joint due to sitting cross-legged for long periods and a subjective feeling of that condition as unpleasant. In refining mindfulness, one learns to differentiate between physical sensations or sounds and how one feels about them, thereby enabling one to dwell in a keenly responsive but less reactive state of mind.

Mr. Goenka told us to notice how even the most stubborn sensations and feelings came and went. I found that if I probed deeply into a piercing pain in the knee, at a certain point it would "switch" from being something solid and unpleasant into a rapidly vibrating pattern of sensations that no longer hurt as much. I realized that what I experienced at any given moment was cocreated by the physical processes of my body and the way I was conditioned to interpret and react to them. I remember a time when I was seated cross-legged outside on the grass between meditation sessions in an ecstatic, silent, openhearted awareness while the gusts of wind rising from the plains of the Punjab below Dharamsala seemed to blow through me. The sense of a separate world "out there" being observed by a detached subject "in here" began to break down.

All this took place more than forty years ago, but its impact remains with me today. It was my initiation into mindfulness, which has been the basis of my contemplative life ever since. Far more than just a technique, mindfulness offered me a new sensibility on life as a whole, an entirely other perspective on how to be a practicing human in the world.

My Tibetan Buddhist education and training during the two years before the retreat had been an ideal preparation for this practice. I was used to spending much of each day cross-legged on the floor, so long hours of sitting meditation did not trouble me. My daily reflections and studies—on the preciousness of human life, the imminence of death, renunciation, existential commitment, an altruistic resolve, and emptiness—provided a fertile soil of value and meaning for mindful awareness to take root in. I had thought deeply about impermanence and selflessness. Now I was experiencing them viscerally. I found myself part of the living fabric of human experience into which I was inseparably woven yet was at the same time free to examine and explore. Mindfulness, I discovered, was not an aloof, detached regard. Its practice served to sculpt and shape the inner contours of my solitude.

Nor was the idea of mindfulness new to me. For many months I had been studying Śāntideva's *A Guide to the Bodhisattva's Way of Life.* The entire fifth chapter of this eighth-century Indian Buddhist text is devoted to the practice of mindful awareness.

Mr. Goenka provided the tools to turn Śāntideva's teachings on mindfulness into a felt reality, while Śāntideva's reflections provided an ethical dimension for Mr. Goenka's contemplative practice. "If the elephant of my mind," wrote Śāntideva, "is firmly bound on all sides by the rope of mindfulness, all fears will cease to exist and all virtues will come into my hand." The purpose of mindfulness is not just to be more aware of the breath, bodily sensations, and feelings. For Śāntideva it means to be constantly mindful of one's ethical aspirations. Mindfulness is compared to the gatekeeper at the doorway of the mind and senses, alert to any impulse that threatens to divert you from your goals and undermine you.

"The thieves of unawareness," he remarks, "follow upon the decline of mindfulness and rob you of your goodness." They circle around "waiting for an opportunity" to break in and take possession of you. Mindfulness is a heightened attention that notices the very first stirring of reactive impulses and neurotic habits before they have a chance to take hold. "When, on the verge of acting, I see my mind is tainted," Śāntideva tells himself, "I should remain immobile, like a piece of wood."

The piece of wood is a metaphor for equanimity, not indifference. Mindfulness is a balanced, reflective stance in which one notices the meanness or sarcasm that rises up in the mind while neither identifying with it nor rejecting it. One observes with interest what is happening without succumbing to either the urge to act on it or the guilty desire to ignore or suppress it. This entails a radical acceptance of who and what you are, where nothing is unworthy of being the object of such attention. You say "yes" to your life as it manifests, warts and all, with an ironic, compassionate regard. Through sustaining this nonreactive stance over time, mindful awareness becomes the basis for one's ethical life.

This perspective is spelled out in the fourteenth-century Tibetan lama Thogmé Zangpo's commentary to Śāntideva's text. For Thogmé Zangpo, mindfulness is "the recollection of all one aspires to let go of and realize," while awareness is "knowing how to do that letting go and realizing." Mindful awareness thus encompasses the entire project of human flourishing. To be mindful means to remember to let go of compulsive reactivity and realize a nonreactive way of life, while to be aware means to know how to refine the psychological, contemplative, philosophical, and ethical skills needed to achieve these goals.

Ever since the Vipassanā retreat with Mr. Goenka and the study of Śāntideva's *A Guide to the Bodhisattva's Way of Life,* the contemplative and ethical dimensions of mindfulness have been inseparable for me. Mindful awareness both embeds my attention in the raw immediacy of experience and serves as the moral compass that guides my response to that experience. "What is the power of mindfulness?" asked Gotama more than a thousand years before Śāntideva. "The noble practitioner is mindful: she is equipped with the keenest mindfulness and awareness; she re-members well and keeps in mind what has been said and done long ago."

13

Wrong-minded people voice opinions,

as do truth-minded people too.

When an opinion is offered, the sage is not drawn in—

there's nothing arid about the sage.

FOUR EIGHTS, 2:1

"I feel death," says Montaigne, "continuously nipping at my throat and kidneys." Montaigne knows that "each stumble of a horse, each falling of a tile, each slight pin prick" could be the harbinger of his end. To be able to die at peace, a philosopher needs to die to his attachments to the world. This, for Montaigne, is "true solitude," where one's thoughts and emotions are reined in and brought under control. "To prepare oneself for death is to prepare oneself for freedom. The one who has learned to die has unlearned to be a slave."

To die to the world is far from straightforward. "People do not recognize the natural sickness of their mind," says Montaigne, which does nothing but "ferret about in search of something, ceaselessly twisting, elaborating, and entangling itself in its own activity like a silkworm, until it suffocates there like 'a mouse in pitch.' " We rush around in a compulsive flight from death. "Every moment," he remarks, "it seems I am fleeing from myself." No matter how many laws or precepts we use to fence the mind in, we still find it "garrulous and dissolute, escaping all constraints." This flight is chaotic and aimless. There is "no madness or lunacy that cannot be produced in this turmoil. When the soul has no definite goal, it gets lost."

Chronic dissatisfaction further drives this restlessness. "Nothing that we know and enjoy feels satisfying," remarks Montaigne.

> Since what is present fails to gratify us, we hanker after future things of which we know nothing. It is not that what is present is unable to gratify us but we grasp it in a sick and uncontrolled way.

This strategy increases the dissatisfaction it seeks to dispel. For what we cling to turns out to be hollow and empty. "We clutch at everything," he says, "but clasp nothing but wind."

Montaigne suggests that nature distracts us from ourselves "so as not to discourage us." To divert our attention, it has "very cleverly projected the activity of our gaze outward so that we are swept forward on its current." This is why "to turn the course of our life back toward us is a painful move." It is hard work to swim against the stream. It creates turbulence, like "when the sea, pushed back onto itself, churns in confusion."

Montaigne compares himself to "a vessel that disintegrates, splits apart, leaks, and shirks its duty to itself. It needs to be knocked together and tightened up with some good strokes of a mallet." Such reform cannot be done piecemeal. It requires a continual training of the soul. "Recover your mind and your will, which are busying themselves elsewhere," he urges. "You are draining away and scattering yourself. Concentrate yourself; hold yourself back. You are being betrayed, dissipated, robbed."

"It is a tricky business," he acknowledges, "to follow so meandering a course as that of our mind, to penetrate its opaque depths and hidden recesses, to discern and stop so many subtle shifts in its movements." This is impossible without rigorous self-governance. To rein in its compulsive wandering, "no beast more justly needs to be given blinkers to keep its gaze focused on what lies before its feet." It requires that you learn how to "keep yourself settled, straight, inflexible, without movement or agitation." "Others," he comments, "study themselves in order to advance and elevate their mind: I seek to humble it and lie it down to rest."

"The procedure that works well for me," says Montaigne, is this: "With very little effort I stop the first movement of my emotions, and let go of whatever has started to weigh me down before it carries me off." By "spying closely on the effects and circumstances of the passions that govern me," he has learned to detect "the tiny breezes that brush against me and murmur inside me, as forerunners of the storm." Seeing them approach lets him "slow down a little the frenzy of their charge." Experience has taught him that without knowing how to "close the door against your emotions, you will never chase them out once they have gained entry."

To succeed in examining and managing one's life is, for Montaigne, to have accomplished the "greatest task of all." It is not easy, but with practice you can tame the mind. Rarely does anyone attempt, let alone succeed in, this endeavor. Montaigne considers himself unusual in this regard: "Never has someone prepared himself to leave the world more simply and totally, or detached himself from it more completely than I strive to do."

Montaigne follows Plato's "middle road" between "hatred of pain and love of pleasure," and instructs himself to "contemplate both pain and pleasure with an equally calm gaze." To live this way, you need to jettison even the guidelines and pointers that have brought you to this point. "Most people get it wrong," he explains.

> Of course one can proceed more easily by sticking to the side of the road, whose curb serves as a limit and a guide, than by following the wide and open middle way. Yes, it is far easier to proceed by artificial than by natural means, but it is far less noble too and held in less esteem. The soul's greatness lies not so much in reaching lofty heights and making progress as in knowing and respecting its range.

One needs to cultivate an intuitive sense of balance and orientation that is responsive to the demands of each moment. "I want death to find me planting my cabbages," he says, "worrying about neither it nor my imperfect garden."

14

I am in a large public art gallery. People are milling around and talking in hushed voices. Behind me is a life-size standing figure that looks like a man encased in lead. On entering the room, I recognized it as a work of the British artist Antony Gormley. The figure leans slightly backward, its arms and legs splayed, its barely discernible features gazing skyward. Called *Untitled (for Francis),* it evokes the moment St. Francis of Assisi received the stigmata, as portrayed in a late-fifteenth-century painting by Giovanni Bellini.

With my back to the ecstatic saint, I gaze at the only other work in the room. It is a five-foot-square abstract painting called *Faraway Love* by the American artist Agnes Martin. It consists of horizontal lines: five thin bands of white and four wider bands of pale blue. The bands are rectangles of different widths, their borders marked by hand-drawn pencil lines.

The paint is applied as a wash. The artist's fingerprints are visible in places. The bottom blue band bears the seemingly accidental mark of a thin streak of blue pigment.

Agnes Martin maintained that her paintings were complete only when they evoked in the viewer the same quality that inspired her to paint them. As I peer at this work, I do not experience love, either close or faraway. I am restless and uncertain as I try to make sense of what I am seeing. Nothing on the canvas holds my attention. I find myself distracted and bored. Perhaps my guilty obligation to appreciate *Faraway Love* undermines the innocent openness of heart required to experience love.

For twenty years Agnes Martin worked in New York and New Mexico as an obscure artist of figurative, landscape, and semi-abstract painting. During this period, she routinely burned most of her work. One day in her early fifties she found herself thinking of the innocence of trees, and a grid of fine vertical lines and pale horizontal bands appeared in her mind. She painted what she saw and titled it *The Tree.*

For the remaining forty years of her life, nearly all her paintings would be squares divided by abstract bands of color wash and penciled lines. Her method was simple and inflexible. She would wait for moments of inspiration in which a tiny square image appeared in her mind. She would scale this up mathematically to the size of the canvas and then reproduce it exactly. She insisted that these paintings transcended the concrete world of sense experience. They were expressions of pure abstract emotion, such as innocence, perfection, benevolence, happiness, and love.

"I paint with my back to the world," she told an interviewer in 1997. She had no interest in what others might think of what she was doing. She denied that these almost featureless works had anything to do with the prairies of Canada, where she was born, or the deserts of New Mexico, where she lived. Nor was she trying to *represent* the feelings that inspired her. By becoming a selfless channel for inspiration, she sought to *reveal* them. Since her paintings originated in inspiration, she refused to take any credit for the finished works. She accepted only the blame for their failure.

Agnes Martin pursued her art with the single-minded dedication of an ascetic. She believed that you have to get rid of everything in life that interferes with your primary inspiration and vision. If this alienates your family and friends, then so be it. For her, ideas, calculations, and ambitions obscure the "sublime, absolute perfection" of life that is present each moment. And the very worst thing you can think of when you are working is yourself. For as soon as the dragon of pride rears its fiery head, she observed, you start making mistakes.

"The best things in life," said Agnes, "happen to you when you're alone." She never married, lived with a partner, or had children. Solitude was the site of her inspiration. She spent months by herself driving around North America in a camper van. For nearly a decade, she settled on the Portales mesa above the New Mexico town of Cuba, without electricity or telephone. The nearest neighbor was six miles away. "A mystic and a solitary person," she wrote, "are the same." Her religion was just "solitude and independence for a free mind."

For years Agnes practiced meditation twenty minutes twice a day in order to still her mind for inspiration. At the age of eighty-five, she declared in a video interview that she no longer meditated because she had learned to stop thinking. "Now," she said,

> I don't think of anything. Nothing goes through my mind. I don't have any ideas myself and I don't believe anybody else's, so that leaves me a clear mind. Gosh, yes, an empty mind, so that when something comes into it you can see it.

The video shows her at work: an old woman with close-cropped hair, a paintbrush in one hand, waddling patiently between the table with her dish of paint and the canvas mounted against a studio wall. She addresses the interviewer with emphatic, chuckling enthusiasm. Her eyes sparkle from a kind, wrinkled face. Now and again they seem to flash with a glint of almost feral wariness. Agnes Martin fought to realize her artistic vision in a male-dominated art world, in a society prejudiced against and frightened of her homosexuality and schizophrenia.

Martin's work has been said to have "the quality of a religious utterance, almost a form of prayer." Agnes inhabited that indefinable space between artistic practice and ascetic practice. Her paintings are infused with the quiet, spacious spirituality of Taoism, Zen, and the Native American culture of New Mexico. To fully appreciate *Faraway Love,* I suspect, you would need to contemplate it over time, ideally alone and in silence.

Antony Gormley, whose figure *Untitled (for Francis)* stood behind me as I reflected on *Faraway Love,* was raised a Catholic and grew up in England. In his early twenties he traveled to India, where he spent three years studying Buddhism. He regards the first ten-day Vipassanā retreat he attended with S. N. Goenka in Dalhousie in 1972 as "the single most important experience of my life." In conversation with the art historian Ernst Gombrich in 1995, he described how meditating on "the sensation of being in a body" became a tool he then transferred to making sculpture. He insists that his sculptures do not *represent* the body but *reveal* the space the body inhabits. Meditation would also have helped him remain still and calm enough while he had his own body cast for works such as *Untitled (for Francis)*. Imagine the solitude of the naked artist wrapped in cling film and two layers of plaster and jute cloth, breathing through straws.

15

It is nine o'clock on a dark, cold evening in December. Fourteen men and women are seated in a medicine circle. Salvador, our shaman, must be about forty. He has short black hair and the beginnings of a moustache and beard. He wears a plain white cotton shirt and trousers. The spacious attic room we are sitting in is illuminated by candlelight. We can hear the insistent rush of the mountain stream that runs beside the farmhouse. We each sit on bedding of some sort: sleeping bags, yoga mats, sheepskins, air mattresses, blankets. On the floor beside each person is a roll of paper towels, a few biodegradable plastic bags, and a bottle of water.

We begin by declaring our motives for being here. I tell Salvador and the others much the same as I told Don Toño above Tepoztlán: I see this ceremony as a way of taking stock of my life. I want to revisit my formative experiences with psychedelics but in sacralized settings using traditional plant medicines. I wish to build on my experience with peyote in Mexico to explore further how these medicines might or might not have a role in today's world.

In his kitchen Salvador has cooked up the ingredients of ayahuasca from the vine *Banisteriopsis caapi* and the leaves of the plant *Psychotria viridis*. The resultant brew is a black liquid, which he has decanted into a large plastic water bottle. We are invited to come up to him one by one. I kneel on the floor and take in both hands the half-glass of ayahuasca he offers me. It has an immediately familiar taste that I cannot identify. Licorice perhaps. And it is not as unpleasant as I feared. Nonetheless, I eat a piece of crystallized ginger to mask the taste, and sip some water.

I sit cross-legged with my eyes shut. After about twenty minutes I feel the distant buildup of a dull, buzzing sensation throughout my body. This is neither pleasant nor unpleasant, and entirely physical. It has no impact on my state of mind, which remains detached, curious, and mildly apprehensive. Before long, intricate, snaking patterns in bright electric colors weave behind my closed eyelids. I peer into their vortices that seem to go on forever. I dislike being subject to intrusive mental content over which I have no control.

I feel flushes of heat and start to sweat. I want to be sick. I detach one of the plastic bags and hold it to my mouth. I retch violently three or four times without disgorging anything. Then I manage to vomit and quickly feel better. This purging seems to eliminate the swirling visual effects and lets me settle into an intensely lucid and collected state of contemplation. Now I am no longer a passive observer of what is happening but an enraptured participant.

I lose count of the number of times I vomit that night. Four? Five? Six? At one point I also have to void my bowels with a splattering blast of gas and diarrhea. The muscles in my sides hurt from retching. The last episode is agony. I retch and retch until I disgorge two loads of bland fluid with the density of mucus. After that I vomit no more and come to rest in an ecstatic solitude. I tremble with cold and curl up under my sleeping bag to keep warm.

With the side of my face pressed against a cushion, I look wide-eyed at the scene from floor level with equanimity. Most of the participants are lying down, inert like me. I listen to my inner monologue reiterate the tiresome story of "that clever asshole who writes books." I repeat this phrase to myself, chuckling quietly. I used to think of "asshole" as a term of abuse. It is but an accurate description of a medium-sized social animal who survives by consuming and evacuating. I think: how wonderful would it be for my *Doppelgänger* to vanish, leaving just *this*.

Salvador is singing in Spanish, accompanying himself on guitar. The music draws me in, piloting me among intricate ravines through which I glide like a bird. His voice stirs me from my trance and I sit up enlivened. Intermittently the song is interrupted by a person retching, followed by clapping, laughter, and cheers. We stand and sway to the music, entering into an unspoken communion. Some couples chastely embrace. No one talks. The shaman's singing fills the silence among us.

At 8:30 a light breakfast of herbal tea, raisins, nuts, and slices of apples appears. We then spend an hour of drawing with colored pencils. I inscribe the Pali word *viveka* (solitude) onto a sheet of paper in Roman script. Carefully following the contours of the letters, I trace concentric lines of different colors around *viveka* until the word radiates a multilayered halo.

16

The eighth-century Chinese Zen teacher Mazu Daoyi once said:

> All of you should realize that your own mind is Buddha. *This* mind is Buddha's mind. You who seek the truth should realize there is nothing to seek. There is no Buddha but mind; no mind but Buddha.

Mazu's point is simple. He's saying that whatever you seek to achieve in meditation is already right here before your eyes. As soon as you use words like "Buddha" or "enlightenment" or "truth," you tend to imagine something far away from the situation you find yourself in now. Mazu tells us that these things are found only in the very midst of what it means to be human in this moment. They are not located anywhere else. Nor, he is saying, are they hidden somewhere in another dimension of your psyche. They are right here in the messiness, confusion, darkness, and anxiety of the very mind that is reading these words.

And, I might add, the body of the Buddha is nothing but the very body that sits on your cushion, its heart beating, its lungs drawing and exhaling each breath, its knees aching from sitting cross-legged. Stop making a difference between who you think you are and who you think the Buddha is.

Mazu was once asked, "What is the meaning of Buddhism?" He retorted, "What is the meaning of this moment?" Try and drop every notion you have formed about the Buddha and Buddhism. Get rid of any thoughts you might have of enlightenment. Instead, just be still, pay attention to what you experience here and now, and let yourself be drawn into the mystery of simply being human, the puzzle of being here at all.

What is this thing you're experiencing right now in all of its stripped-bare vulnerability, ineffability, banality? What is that? What is this thing that was thrust into the world at birth? This thing that will get sick, that will get old, that will die. What is it? Let go of any answers to this question that you may have acquired from Buddhism or elsewhere. Put all such thoughts out of your mind.

The practice of Zen is about coming to terms with the question of who and what you are. Allow yourself to be a mystery for yourself rather than a set of more or less interesting facts. Most human beings at certain moments in their lives experience something like this. It might happen through being in nature, through art, through falling in love, through practicing philosophy, in coming close to death. At any moment when you are suddenly overwhelmed by the fact that you are here at all, rather than not here.

When you ask, "What is this?" do not narrow the sense of "this" just to what is palpable within the confines of your own skin. "This" includes the totality of what is present in this moment: what's arising from within, and what's going on all around you. One might even say it is what is prior to the distinction between self and other, you and me, you and the world. Before I think that I am here and you are there. Something primordial, like the sense of the world an unformed child might have.

Zen practice is about opening yourself to this mystery, allowing yourself to become totally immersed in the perplexity or wonder it evokes, so that it begins to suffuse your consciousness as a whole, not just when you're meditating. Whether you're sitting cross-legged on a cushion or peeling potatoes in the kitchen, notice how utterly strange all this is. Let the astonishment take hold of you more and more and become part of your felt sense of being in the world. Questioning infuses your awareness. Experience comes alive in a startling and puzzling way.

I find myself utterly incapable of putting what it is I'm experiencing right now into words. I do not know what on earth is going on here. The practice of "What is this?" confronts you with what philosophers call the sheer "facticity" of your existence. This is the inescapable reality of what it's like to be me, which seems impossible to articulate or define.

This is an embodied inquiry. When you first ask, "What is this?" in meditation, the question may have little traction on how you feel in your body. It might seem just a curious mental exercise. It might not grab you viscerally at all. But over time, as you settle into a quieter, more lucid awareness, this perplexity begins to resonate and reverberate through your nerves, flesh, bones, and skin.

Don't expect anything to happen. Just wait. This waiting is a deep acceptance of the moment as such. Nietzsche called it *amor fati*—unquestioning love of whatever has fated you to be here. You reach a point where you're just sitting there, asking, "What is this?"—but with no interest in an answer. The longing for an answer compromises the potency of the question. Can you be satisfied to rest in this puzzlement, this perplexity, in a deeply focused and embodied way? Just waiting without any expectations?

Ask "What is this?," then open yourself completely to what you "hear" in the silence that follows. Be open to this question in the same way as you would listen to a piece of music. Pay total attention to the polyphony of the birds and wind outside, the occasional plane that flies overhead, the patter of rain on a window. Listen carefully, and notice how listening is not just an opening of the mind but an opening of the heart, a vital concern or care for the world, the source of what we call compassion or love.

17

On Monday, February 5, 2001, a Chilean Navy patrol boat deposited Robert Kull and a kitten on a tiny, uninhabited, rain-and-wind-lashed island off the southern tip of Patagonia. Once his building materials and crates of supplies were unloaded on the beach, the boat departed. It was getting dark. Bob hauled some timber and plywood to higher ground, made a platform for his tent, put the kitten inside a cardboard box, and settled down for the night. At fifty-four, he intended to spend a year here alone. The nearest human habitation was Puerto Natales, sixty miles away across impassable mountains and fjords.

Bob had been alone in wilderness before. In his late twenties, he'd left his logging job, bought a canoe, and paddled off into the Canadian outback for three months. "Deep solitude," he wrote later, "is strange and powerful and can often be frightening. I almost lost it out there in northern British Columbia. Without other people to help me maintain my identity, the façade of autonomous self-sufficiency started to crumble." This existential meltdown precipitated an ecstatic experience of mystical union with nature that lasted for several weeks. It was then that he decided that one day he would spend a year by himself in nature.

The island on which Bob found himself was as remote as possible from other human beings. From his cabin he looked out at nothing but sand, ocean, rocks, trees, clouds, mountains, and glaciers. No boats ever passed by. No fishermen, hunters, or backpackers would disturb him. Apart from a government official who came to check on him once, he might just as well have been on the moon.

Bob recorded his experiment in radical aloneness in a journal. He soon admitted that "daily writing feels like breaking solitude."

> The voice of solitude must, in some sense, remain silent. As soon as the solitary begins to speak, even if by writing to an imagined reader, he (or she) is no longer truly alone.

The problem is not so much the writing, "but thinking beforehand about what I'll write. When I do that I'm not really here in solitude, but in an imaginary future where someone else is reading my descriptions." Yet whenever he considers not writing, "I'm hit with a wave of isolation, and loneliness."

The journal recounts the construction and maintenance of his cabin, ongoing issues with a wind generator, solar panels, a wood-burning stove, and outboard motors, worries about fresh water, firewood, blackflies, and shoulder pains, observations of condors, eagles, ducks, dolphins, seals, and limpets, comments about books he's reading, and a great deal of fishing. As his time alone unfolds, the sea, the landscape, and the weather assume complex, shifting moods and the kitten is anthropomorphized into Cat. Bob settles into a routine of meditation, philosophical introspection, writing poems, and taking photographs. After six weeks he was able to write: "I saw jet contrails for the first time yesterday far away over the mountains, but it didn't seem to affect me. I don't have a sense of super solitude. I'm just here. It's where I live now."

Bob belongs to a restless frontier culture. He seems at home in the untethered American spirituality that goes back to Emerson and Thoreau, William James and Walt Whitman. For inspiration he draws from the *I Ching,* Zhuangzi, Rumi, Thomas Merton, Jiddu Krishnamurti, Alan Watts, Ken Wilber, Joseph Goldstein, Mary Oliver, and Mihaly Csikszentmihalyi. He earnestly seeks a psychospiritual fulfillment that somehow abolishes the ego. "To be fully human," he writes, "we need relationship not only with other people but with the nonhuman world, with our own inner depths—and with Something Greater. For me, that nonmaterial Presence is mysterious and sacred. It can be experienced, but not defined." His words echo with a yearning to recover in solitude a living connection with what used to be called God.

He quotes a passage from Merton, a Trappist monk: "The hermit's whole life is a life of silent adoration. His very solitude keeps him ever in the presence of God. His whole day, in the silence of his cell, or his garden looking out upon the forest, is a prolonged communion." Bob is not convinced. "This was written by a man who either had his head up his ass or was bullshitting the public," he remarks. From all Bob's extensive reading, "nowhere does Merton's statement find support."

On the contrary. The mind and heart are all over the place, from the most trivial, mundane, and negative to the joyful, peaceful, and sacred. Solitude is like the rest of life, only with less opportunity for escape into diversion.

There is something banal and everyday about solitude. Even in company we spend much of our time alone, absorbed in our innermost thoughts and feelings, quietly talking to ourselves. Whether we live in Manhattan or the middle of nowhere, this is our condition.

As I reread his journal and study the photo gallery on his website, an image of Bob as the last man on earth comes to haunt me. Yes, there is great beauty and joy in wilderness, but only when you know it can be shared with others. Were Bob the only survivor of an Armageddon, I suspect his Patagonian solitude would be an intolerable loneliness devoid of meaning. Bob may have physically cut himself off from humankind, but he still had email. He used it to send coded signs of life to his friends once a month and get technical support on waterlogged outboard motors. Likewise, his friends agonized over whether to tell him about the 9/11 attacks in New York. (They chose not to.) This invisible umbilical cord bound him irrevocably to a human community.

"Perhaps the most useful aspect of my year alone in the wilderness," he wrote to me some years later, in 2017, "was to come to accept that my inner world has its own inherent weather patterns, as does the external world. The recognition that I'm not in control and that gray days do not mean I've done something wrong. That all the ups and downs, lights and darks, are part of who I am; who we are."

18

One who takes no issue with things

sees what's before his eyes, is open to what is said,

acts in tune with what he senses.

Who can judge him here? By what measure?

FOUR EIGHTS, 3:6

In 1554, King Henry II commanded a fleet to establish a settlement for French Protestants in Brazil, a land discovered and claimed by Portugal in the first year of the century. On November 10, 1555, the French landed on an island in Guanabara Bay and proceeded to build a fort. This was to serve as the base for a colony called "French Antarctica." Five years later, the Portuguese evicted them. On returning to France, one of them—possibly a sailor from Bordeaux—went into service at Michel de Montaigne's estate.

Montaigne describes him as "a simple and rough man—good qualities for telling the truth." He learns from him that sickness is rare among the people of Brazil and one never sees a person "trembling, bleary, toothless, or bent over with age." The Indians attribute their good health and longevity to the serenity and tranquility of the air. Montaigne thinks it has to do with "the tranquility and serenity of their souls." These people are "barbarous," he says, only in that they have been "little influenced by the human intellect and are still very close to their original simplicity."

Montaigne imagines telling Plato that "this is a nation with no commerce of any kind, no knowledge of writing, no understanding of numbers, no idea of magistrates or political rank, no use of servants, no wealth or poverty, no contracts, no inheritances, no divisions of property, only leisurely occupations, no concern for any kinship except mutual respect for one another, no clothes, no agriculture, no metals, no use of wine or corn. How far from such perfection would Plato find the Republic he imagined."

He depicts here a Garden of Eden inhabited by people Seneca describes as "fresh from the hands of the gods." They naturally enjoy the ease and leisure Montaigne values in his solitude. These unclothed Indians are already empty of the presumption and opinion that plague us. Montaigne yearns for such innocence: "I want to be seen," he says, "in my simple, natural, and ordinary guise, unstudied and without artifice. . . . Had I found myself among those people who are said still to live under the sweet liberty of nature's first laws, I can assure you that I would most willingly have depicted myself whole, and wholly naked."

Montaigne's admiration of the natural intelligence of dogs, cats, and horses, his respect for the innate wisdom of peasants, and his love of bathing naked with strangers at spas are vindicated by what he learns of these Indians. He collects their artifacts. "In several places, including my own home, you can see the style of their beds and ropework as well as their wooden swords and the wooden bracelets with which they protect their wrists in battle, and the tall open-ended canes to the sound of which they beat the time of their dances." He tastes their staple food, which resembles "coriander cakes." It is "sweetish and rather bland."

Such was the curiosity about these unknown people that some were shipped to France and paraded around the country. As part of the royal army that retook Rouen from the Protestants in 1562, Montaigne had the opportunity to meet three Indians who were then in the city. He asked them their impressions of France. One of them explained that in their language they call all men "halves" of one another. Here, by contrast, they saw "men filled and gorged with all sorts of good things while their halves were beggars at their doors, emaciated with hunger and poverty." They found it strange that "those destitute halves would suffer such injustice, and did not take the others by the throat or set their houses on fire."

On learning of the Spanish conquests of Mexico and Peru, Montaigne is horrified at the "trickery and sleight of hand," the brutality and unbridled greed of the conquistadores. "It was an infant world," he says, "and we whipped it into submission to our doctrines and disciplines." Uninvited, the Spaniards burst into its solitude and shattered it. Yet the way these people conducted themselves in negotiations revealed them to be "in no way inferior to us in their natural clarity of mind and sense of justice." As for "piety, observance of laws, goodness, generosity, loyalty, and sincerity, it served us well not to have had as much as they. By surpassing us in these virtues, they ruined, sold, and betrayed themselves."

On reading of the magnificence of the cities of Cuzco and Mexico, the great highway from Quito to Cuzco, the outstanding workmanship in precious stones and painting, Montaigne deplores the destruction of those civilizations. "So many towns razed to the ground, so many nations exterminated, so many millions of people put to the sword, the most beautiful and richest part of the world turned upside down: all for the sake of trading in pearls and pepper." It shocks him how the Spaniards "not merely confess to these deeds, they boast of them far and wide." And this genocide was justified because "the Pope, God's representative on earth, had granted dominion over all the Indies."

Montaigne recounts that the king of Peru "was condemned to be publicly hanged and strangled, after first being compelled to buy off the agony of being burned alive by accepting baptism." "Oh why," he asks himself, "did it not fall to Alexander or those ancient Greeks and Romans to make of this a most noble conquest?" Such men "would have gently refined those peoples, clearing away whatever savagery there was, while encouraging and cultivating the good seeds that nature had sown in them. . . . What a renewal that would have been, what an improvement of the world, if the first examples of our behavior presented there had inspired those peoples to admire virtue and to imitate it, and established between them and us a brotherly fellowship and understanding."

19

When the gravely impish Salvador offers me another half-glass of ayahuasca to drink, I shudder. My body recoils at the prospect of consuming something that the evening before had made it violently sick. This time the black liquid tastes horrible and immediately makes me feel nauseous. I eat two pieces of crystallized ginger, but they fail to mask its flavor.

With most psychoactive substances, the effects diminish with repeated use, requiring you to increase the dose. You do not build up a tolerance for ayahuasca. As the medicine takes hold, I realize that it is just as potent as, if not more than, the night before. I dry-heave once, after which the urge to vomit and the swirling visual effects both cease. I occasionally feel a bit queasy, but that's all.

I enter an ecstatic state of contemplation. Whether sitting cross-legged or curled up on my yoga mat, standing upright or padding around the room in my thick winter socks, I commune with the arresting strangeness of ordinary things. I am entranced by the uncomprehending look in my own eyes as I ponder my reflection in a bathroom mirror. I am overwhelmed by the utter beauty of human beings. I gaze raptly at their simplest gestures: placing a hand on a door handle, opening a window, sighing.

The roaring hush of a moonless night bursts through the window, infusing the room with chilled air. I stare at a silver birch, a pale, thin sentinel against the somber forest. An eternity later I return from this intimacy with nature to my fellow humans in the room. The women are intoxicatingly delicate and vulnerable in their movements and faces in a way that is not sexual at all.

Ludwig repeatedly hammers the floor with his fists and writhes about on his mattress. His distress is excruciating. I find this hard to bear and have an urge to leave the room. But no one moves. We stay there, holding Ludwig in our silent embrace. Salvador chants a medicine song while rattling a *chacapa,* a frond of dried maize leaves, over him. The pounding and moaning increase, then slowly lessen until Ludwig is once more at rest.

Oskar crashes to the floor, spewing vomit and diarrhea on his clothes and bedding. Vadik and Carsten rush over with towels and buckets to clean up the mess and comfort him. The candlelit scene in this farmhouse attic changes into Caravaggio's early-seventeenth-century painting *The Crucifixion of St. Peter.* There, in the stark tonal contrasts of chiaroscuro, a bewildered old man, naked but for a loincloth, is nailed to a cross being hoisted from the ground, one man straining with a rope as another with dirty feet crouches below to help push up the load with his shoulder.

Poor Oskar lying in his own filth carries the same numinous weight for me as Peter's martyrdom.

I lie down and am drawn into a meditation on the human eye. I peer into the fine optical structure of the organ itself, marveling at its intricacy and beauty. Looking into an eye means looking into someone's eye. And as your eye in turn regards me, it silently implores, in the words of Emmanuel Levinas: "Do not hurt me." A succession of dear faces passes before me: family, friends, colleagues, students . . . I long for them to be participating in this ceremony too. I am pierced by my love for each one of them. I am suddenly looking into the eyes of the rat I caught in a wire cage that past summer. Those tiny black shining orbs call out: "Please, do me no harm." I feel the guilt and shame of trapping the rat. I will release it in a distant woodland rather than kill it. Yet I know I might have separated a mother from her babies. I know that her chances of survival might be slim outside her own territory. I want to lead a life of complete harmlessness, but I fail.

20

on meditation (*jhāna*)

gotama, the buddha

selected passages from the pali canon

I said to myself: "These painful austerities have not led to any transcendent states, any knowledge or vision able to ennoble one. Could there be another way?"

Then I recalled: "Once, while my father the Sakiyan was at work, I was sitting in the cool shade of a rose-apple tree. Untroubled by sensual desires or unskillful ideas, I entered into and dwelled in the first meditation, which is accompanied by thought and reflection, by rapture and well-being born of solitude. Could that be the way?"

Recalling this, I realized: "Yes, this is the way. Why do I fear a well-being that has nothing to do with sensual desire or unskillful ideas? There is no reason to fear that well-being. Yet it is hard to experience it with a body so emaciated. Why don't I eat some solid food?" So I ate some boiled rice and junket.

Imagine a skilled bath attendant or his apprentice who pours soap powder into a metal basin, sprinkles it with water, and kneads it into a ball, so that the ball of soap is pervaded, encompassed, and suffused with moisture inside and out, yet with no seepage. So the meditator suffuses her body with the rapture and well-being born of solitude, so that no part of her body is not suffused by that rapture and well-being.

Imagine a deep lake whose waters well up from below. It has no inlets for streams from east, from west, from north, from south, nor is it refilled by timely showers of rain. Yet a current of cool water, welling up from within the lake, suffuses the entire body of water, so no part of it is not suffused with cool water. So the meditator suffuses her body with the rapture and well-being born of collectedness, so that no part of her body is not suffused by that rapture and well-being.

Imagine ponds of blue, red, or white lotus flowers that germinated, grew up in, and never rise above the surfaces of those ponds. Such plants thrive underwater. From their tips to their roots they are suffused with cool water, so that no part of them is not suffused with it. So the meditator suffuses her body with well-being devoid of rapture, so that no part of her body is not suffused by that well-being.

Imagine a seated person covered from head to foot by a white cloth, so that no part of her body is untouched by that white cloth. So the meditator sits suffusing her body with a pure bright mind, so that no part of her body is not suffused by that pure bright mind.

Imagine a fine hexagonal crystal, polished, shining, transparent, flawless, strung on a blue, yellow, red, white, or colorless thread. A person with keen sight, taking it in her hand, would reflect: "Here is a fine hexagonal crystal, strung on a blue, yellow, red, white, or colorless thread." So when her mind is collected, pure and bright, the practitioner directs and inclines it to knowing and seeing. She understands: "This is my body, having physical form, composed of four elements, born of father and mother, nourished with rice and broth, impermanent, liable to be broken and destroyed, and this is my consciousness, supported by and bound up with it."

Just as the Ganga slants, slopes, and inclines toward the east, so too a practitioner who develops and cultivates the four meditations slants, slopes, and inclines toward nirvana.

21

Among the work in Vermeer's studio at his death in 1675 was an allegorical painting titled *Schilderkonst* (*The Art of Painting*). A painter, his back turned to the viewer, sits on a stool in front of a canvas that rests on an easel. A young woman in a blue satin dress, clutching a book to her bosom and holding a trumpet in her right hand, poses for him. He has just begun depicting the blue-tinted leaves of her tiara. One post of the easel stands on the tiled floor of alternating black and white squares. The easel's other post is clearly visible above the painter's beret, but where it should emerge onto the floor beside his foot there is nothing. By the laws of physics the easel should not be standing.

It troubles me that the word "art" is the same as in "artifice" and "artificial." I value art as a way of truth-telling. I refuse to think of Agnes Martin's *Faraway Love* as somehow fake. But as I scrutinize the woman in the blue dress in *The Art of Painting,* I feel she is making fun of me. Her fluttering eyelids and the impish slant of her lips suggest she is not taking any of it seriously. This, she seems to say, is just a painting of a painting being painted, an attempt to say something truthful about the manufacture of illusions.

The more I look at Vermeer's paintings, the more theatrical they become. A wealthy merchant's daughter trying on a pearl necklace turns into one of the artist's friends or family members dressed up in fancy clothes and playing a role in a charade. Vermeer makes no attempt to conceal what he is doing. The same props—tables, carpets, chairs, costumes, and wall hangings—are rearranged in what often looks like the same room. As I consider these actors, I detect their complicity with the artist. Some scholars have identified Vermeer with the grinning, rakish figure holding a glass of wine in his early painting *The Procuress*. This reinforces my sense of him as a trickster, a jester, a clown.

Johannes Vermeer and Agnes Martin both painted with their backs to the world. Whether surrounded by noisy children in a townhouse in Delft or alone on a mesa in the high desert of New Mexico, they pursued the same solitary vocation. Both have left behind pigment-coated canvases secured to wooden supports that have achieved iconic if not transcendent significance. Painters and writers need solitude to forge and refine the vision of their art. They pass long stretches of time alone with their work, anonymous, ignored, haunted by the prospect of ridicule or failure. Solitude is a necessary condition for developing their imagination and their craft.

To be alone at your desk or in your studio is not enough. You have to free yourself from the phantoms and inner critics who pursue you wherever you go. "When you start working," said the composer John Cage, "everybody is in your studio—the past, your friends, enemies, the art world, and above all, your own ideas—all are there. But as you continue painting, they start leaving, one by one, and you are left completely alone. Then, if you are lucky, even you leave."

Solitude is considered an aberration. The person who keeps herself apart is labeled "antisocial," a "loner," even a "misanthrope." Solitary confinement is regarded as the worst kind of punishment short of execution. "We have been very strenuously conditioned against solitude," observed Agnes Martin. "To be alone is considered to be a grievous and dangerous condition." She encourages artists to recall times when they were alone and examine carefully their responses to aloneness. She advises them to create opportunities for being by themselves, to avoid unnecessary company, even that of cats and dogs. She suggests that those who enjoy being alone could become "serious workers in the art field."

Having shut the door, you find yourself alone before a canvas, a sheet of paper, a lump of clay, a computer screen. Other tools and materials lie around, close at hand, waiting to be used. You resume your silent conversation with the work. This is a two-way process: you create the work and then you respond to it. The work can inspire, surprise, and shock you. For Martin it is crucial to understand the response you have to your own work, to know how it makes you feel. In this way, "you discover your direction and truth about yourself." The solitary act of making art involves intense, wordless dialogue.

22

In 2016, I participated in two seven-day *jhāna* retreats with the American meditation teacher Leigh Brasington: the first in August in England, the second in December in Portugal. The word *jhāna* in Pali simply means meditation. To distinguish it from other meditations, it is often translated as "absorption." The jhānas describe an arc of four phases of collectedness (*samādhi*), starting with a focused state of rapture and well-being accompanied by reflection and analysis, and culminating in a state of stillness and well-being characterized by lucidity and equanimity. They are presented as ways to stabilize and sharpen the mind in order to see more clearly into the nature of things.

After rejecting the traditional forms of meditation and asceticism current in India at his time, Gotama recalled an experience he'd had as a child. Seated alone beneath a tree, he had suddenly found himself in what he would come to call the "first jhāna." His memory of this ecstatic state led him to regain trust in his own innocent intuition rather than rely on the authority of meditation teachers or established ascetic practices. "Yes," he said to himself, "this is the way." He realized there was nothing wrong with such bliss that arose entirely from within himself. So he resumed the practice of the jhānas until he arrived at an awakening.

Given the centrality of this episode in the life story of the Buddha, it is odd how few Buddhist teachers encourage their students to practice the jhānas. Some will even tell their students to avoid the jhānas because of the risk of getting attached to the pleasurable feelings associated with them. Others present them as such advanced and subtle states of mind that they are effectively unattainable for all but specialists. In my own training, I was never once advised to practice the jhānas. This traditional reticence did not deter the German-born nun Ayya Khema (1923–97), who rediscovered them for herself and then taught them to her students, among whom was the self-styled "ex-hippy computer programmer" Leigh Brasington.

Leigh's instructions for entering the jhānas are simple. You start by focusing on the breath as when practicing mindfulness. You then turn your attention to the sensations on your upper lip created by the passage of inhalations and exhalations. Over time, these sensations coalesce into what feels like a solid, fixed point. Once you can sustain attention on this point for several minutes, you gently smile to yourself and shift your focus to the pleasurable feeling that accompanies the smile. As you dwell on this pleasure in a relaxed and disinterested way, then, as Leigh puts it: "the jhāna will find you."

Almost as soon as I began following Leigh's instructions on the first day of the first retreat, I entered into a calm and steady meditative state. That first night I lay awake with perfect contentment saturating my body. Over the course of the next day, the practice led me to a deep, calm contemplation of the tragic and ephemeral nature of my life, which was sobering and moving. I experienced little distraction while sitting but also no rapture. The pleasant, even blissful feelings that permeated my body/mind were more pronounced when I walked outside, drank tea, or lay down after the sessions of seated meditation than during the sessions themselves.

Doing samādhi practice, I realized, is like gently putting on the brakes and stopping, which allows a whole new perspective to open up with regard to life, based on still, focused bodily joy.

At 11:00 AM on the fourth day, Leigh gave a talk on the tonality of feeling. Seated on a chair, I listened politely. Then I noticed a build-up of sensations in the center of my chest, which started radiating out as an ecstatic flow. I became completely immersed in this as it came forth, sometimes in surges that made me lean forward and sway from side to side. It dawned on me that this must be rapture.

In ordinary concentration, I have to hold my attention on the object, but now it was the rapture, centered in the middle of the chest but also suffusing the body, that held my attention. I didn't have to do anything. At the same time, I was fully conscious of everything else going on around me. This continued uninterrupted until the bell at 12:30 and carried on all through lunch, after which I went to my room to lie down. I lay on my back, took a few deep breaths, as Leigh had advised, and relaxed, which resulted in the rapture's diminishing, leaving me with a suffused, bright contentment, also extending through the entire body.

I went out for a walk in the hamlet of West Ogwell, quietly and beatifically aware of all that I encountered. As I passed by a cottage, I noticed a dog in the yard and went up to stroke it through the bars of the gate. In catching its mournful eye, I was overwhelmed by an upsurge of rapture from the center of my chest, which made me gasp for breath and nearly lose my balance. I stumbled over to a log, on which I sat down to collect myself. The rapture was not as sustained as in the morning but continued as a physical presence that remained with me as I slowly continued my walk. But as soon as I returned to the hall and sat in meditation, it vanished.

If this is jhāna, then jhāna is not (as I had assumed until then) just an intensification of the concentration one develops during Vipassanā or Zen meditation. It is of another order. It shifts one into a different body-mindset altogether. It is a gift. And it is not just a precursor to further insight later but affords another perspective on—and consolidation of—the understanding one has already developed.

That night I slept badly and the next day struggled with the expectation of rapture, which, I suspect, prevented it from happening. I cannot deny that I enjoyed the nonordinary and ecstatic experience of the day before in a way that made me crave to have it again. To provoke it I started smiling more forcefully until, in my mind's eye, the smile turned into a mocking skull's rictus. My low mood made it very difficult to generate any sense of joy—everything I did seemed shallow and artificial.

The second jhāna retreat that winter in Portugal was not as dramatic or eventful as the first. It consolidated my practice of collectedness, making my meditation more grounded, embodied, and still. I settled more and more into an undistractability that remained whatever was going on around me. At times the meditation became very quiet and I felt myself shifting gears, so to speak, as a "vibrating space" of pristine concentration took over. Occasionally, a diffuse white light permeated my awareness. Once I was convinced that I was floating about six feet above the ground. Again, the effects of the meditation were often more apparent outside the formal sessions of sitting. Wandering slowly through the fruit groves around the retreat, I would find myself at rest in a spacious clarity of mind that was more palpable than any of the thoughts and emotions going on within it.

The classical definition of the first jhāna describes it as "born from solitude." To train the mind to dwell in sustained collectedness clearly requires removing oneself from the distractions and pressures of daily life. But this is not enough. The solitude that gives birth to the first jhāna is primarily a state of mind. Such inner solitude is characterized by the delight, ease, and freedom that come from no longer being the puppet of one's desires, aversions, low and high energy levels, doubts, and anxieties. The jhānas, therefore, are a natural consequence of disentangling oneself from the habitual patterns and mood swings that bedevil us.

In one of his talks, Leigh quoted the Buddhist philosopher Nāgārjuna, who said:

> There is no walking without walkers
> And no walkers without walking.

Likewise, there can be no meditation without a meditator, no jhāna without a jhāna practitioner and no jhāna practitioner without a jhāna. And since each jhāna practitioner is a different person, the jhāna experienced by me may be quite different from the jhāna experienced by you.

A jhāna has no independent existence apart from the person doing the practice. It will mean something different depending on the experience, outlook, beliefs, and so on of the meditator. The mutually interdependent relationship between the jhāna and the meditator will give rise to something unpredictable in its specificity. The texts, therefore, can only give us a rough guide, a rule of thumb, as to what the experience of jhāna will be "like."

Rapture and well-being suffuse the body independently of any external sensory input. They may well vary in intensity and kind for each person. The widely differing opinions as to what a jhāna is could simply reflect the different ways and levels at which it resonates for different meditators. Jhāna practice enabled me to recognize and attune myself to the optimal affective and somatic pitch for my contemplative practice.

Nor do scholars agree on what the jhānas are. Toward the end of the retreat in Portugal, I read Israeli scholar Keren Arbel's Ph.D. thesis on the four jhānas. She says: "One attains the jhānas not by fixating the mind or being absorbed into a meditation object but by releasing and letting go of the foothold of unwholesome mind. . . . The four jhānas should not be perceived as a narrow field of awareness, directed on a single point but as an undirected broad field of awareness." For Keren, the jhānas are not trancelike absorptions but the actualization and embodiment of understanding itself.

23

Ayahuasca is sometimes called *La Purga*—the purge. It is tempting to consider the vomiting as a mere side effect of the medicine. As I look back on it now, I consider it an integral and necessary part of the experience. On both evenings, the journey followed a similar arc: the buildup of sensations through the body; the appearance of swirling, colorful patterns; the retching and vomiting; the settling into a lucid, still, equanimous contemplation. This arc starts by a dissolution of one's sense of being a judgmental, anxious observer, followed by the descent into a keen somatic and participatory awareness of everything that is unfolding within and around you.

I doubt that simply ingesting a psychoactive substance like ayahuasca will in itself produce wisdom, love, or enlightenment. The medicine amplifies the values of the culture or religion to which one already belongs. Even without being consciously invoked, such values underwrite the motives for taking the substance and establish the framework for interpreting its effects. Ayahuasca is not a shortcut: it catalyzes, clarifies, and perhaps accelerates a process that is already under way. Ayahuasqueros talk of the sessions as "work." The ceremonies can be challenging and unsettling. More than once have I heard the experience compared to the rebooting of a computer. The chemical reaction that occurs between the alkaloids and your neurotransmitters is only one of many factors that contribute to the overall experience.

Whether practicing meditation or participating in a shamanic ceremony, we release chemicals into our system that affect our state of consciousness. Does it matter whether these chemicals are the dopamine, norepinephrine, or serotonin within our own bodies or the mescaline and dimethyltriptamine that are introduced by ingesting plants? Once we relinquish the idea of a mind or spirit existing independent of the physical body, we need to accept that we are made of the very same molecules that compose the natural world. With the dissolution of the mind-body split that characterizes most religions (including Amazonian shamanism and Buddhism), we embark on a practice that no longer seeks to separate one's self from the physical world but joyously embraces that world as part of who and what we are.

As I sit in the train on my way back to Bordeaux thirty-six hours after taking the last dose, the effects of the medicine are still present in a gentle but palpable way. I feel neither physically drained nor mentally depleted. My sense of the world and its creatures is infused with an empathetic curiosity and a bright, exalted attention. My background anxiety and the annoying worries it generates have all but evaporated. I am nonetheless queasy and have not yet regained much appetite for food. Each time I cough, the muscles in my sides ache from retching. I can taste a faint acid reflux in the back of my throat and nostrils.

Following Salvador's instructions, I continue to fast for three days after the ceremony. I eat less and avoid meat, cheese, wine, onions, garlic, and coffee. The day before the end of the fast I resolve not to drink alcohol anymore. This is not a moral but a bodily decision. After years of drinking wine most evenings, I suddenly find that a glass of Saint-Estèphe holds no attraction. The medicine has enabled me to relate to alcohol from a completely other perspective. I find the idea of consuming it not so much repellent as perplexing.

The next days, whenever I see a good bottle of wine, I still think: "I'd like a glass of that." But the idea is not followed by a bodily impulse to act on it. No visceral tug of longing occurs. The thought no longer triggers desire. In the following months, such thoughts faded away too. I continued to enjoy the bodily feeling of *not* drinking. I felt as though a muscular grip had been loosened, opening an inner sluice gate that released feelings of lightness, contentment, and ease.

I did not consider my drinking to be problematic, though I readily admit that I might have been deluding myself. My motives for attending the ceremony did not include a desire to renounce wine. The most unexpected consequence of having taken ayahuasca is to have been purged of that habit. Ayahuasca achieved something in forty-eight hours that government health warnings and Buddhist moralizing had failed to do over decades. In June 2019, as I finalize this manuscript for publication, I am aware that I have not drunk a drop of alcohol for more than two and a half years.

24

on presumption

michel de montaigne

selected passages from the essays

I am very ignorant about what I am. I marvel at the assurance and confidence people have of themselves— while there is hardly anything I know for sure and that I could guarantee being able to do. I do not possess a checklist of my abilities; I learn about them only after they have done their job.

Philosophy never plays a more beautiful game than when it counters our presumption and vanity; when it frankly recognizes its own indecisiveness, weakness, and igno- rance. The wet nurse who breastfeeds the most delusive opinions, both public and private, is the inordinately good opinion one has of oneself.

I consider myself a typical sort of person, except insofar as I consider myself so.

My palate is sensitive and hard to please: especially about me. I always disapprove of myself. In every situation I feel myself drifting and yielding with weakness. I have nothing of my own that can satisfy my tastes.

No matter how many times I go over my own writings, rather than pleasing me they disappoint and irritate me. I always have an idea in my mind, a fuzzy image, of a far better expression than the one I used, but, like in a dream, I can neither grasp nor develop it.

I know how to neither please, delight, nor titillate; the best tale in the world dries up in my hands and drones on. I know only how to talk seriously. I am quite devoid of that facility, which I see in several of my acquaintances, to chat away with every newcomer, keep an audience on the edge of its seats, or engage a prince on all sorts of topics without boring him.

I have a sluggish and blunt mind: a mere wisp of cloud stops it in its tracks. My understanding is slow and confused, but once it has grasped something, it holds on to it well, embracing it completely, tightly, and deeply.

Being unable to control events, I control myself: I adjust myself to them if they do not adjust themselves to me.

I like my misfortunes to be unalloyed, those that don't stress or trouble me further about whether they can be sorted out but from the outset plunge me straight into suffering.

The lowest step is the most firm: it is the seat of constancy. Being its own foundation, it rests entirely on itself.

Truth is the first and fundamental part of virtue. It must be loved for its own sake.

By nature my soul refuses to lie and hates even to think of it. I suffer an internal shame and stabbing remorse if a lie escapes me, as it sometimes does when circumstances force me to improvise.

That is why I surrender to candor: both naturally and by inclination I always say what I think—and leave the outcome in the hands of Fortune. Aristippus said the principal benefit he drew from philosophy was to speak freely and openly to everyone.

So I stay with my doubts and my freedom to choose until the situation forces me to decide. Then, to tell the truth, I usually "throw the feather to the wind," as they say, and surrender myself to the mercies of Fortune: letting the slightest whim or circumstance carry me off.

The uncertainty of my judgment is so equally balanced on most oc-casions that I would happily resort to deciding by dice or the toss of a coin.

In my own conduct I make little use of my intelligence: I readily let myself be led by the usual order of this world. Happy are those who do what they are told rather than tell others what to do, who do not agonize about the causes of things but let themselves gently roll along with the rolling of the heavens.

People always look at what faces them: me, I turn my gaze inside. I plant it there, I harbor it there. Everyone looks ahead. Me, I look inside. I deal only with myself. I think about myself incessantly, I regulate myself, I taste myself.

Maybe due to my ongoing contact with the humors of the ancients and the impression I have of those enriched souls of the past, I am disgusted both with myself and others. In truth, we live in an age that produces only mediocrity.

The kind of people least worthy of disdain are those who by the sim-plicity of their nature take the lowest position. They offer us a more honest encounter. I find that the customs and views of peasants con-form better to the teaching of true philosophy than those of our philosophers.

25

I was ill-prepared that autumn for the hike up to Baekun Am, the hermitage on White Cloud Mountain. The rain had started as a fine drizzle early that morning and was now a constant, sullen downpour. On leaving the main temple in the valley below, our group of pilgrims branched off the road onto a steep and narrow path in the forest. We were soon pushing our way through dripping foliage. My clothes were soaked, and my light town shoes slipped and squelched as we climbed. I was cold and irritated.

Koreans, like the British, cheerfully ignore inclement weather. After a number of turns onto trails that petered out—all occasions for much mirth—we clambered down a precipitous rocky path that took us to the tiny hermitage. The clouds were parting, and hesitant patches of sunlight illuminated the pine trees that disappeared into the mist below. On a stony patch of flat ground at the top of a ravine beneath a sheer cliff of pale rock, Baekun Am was just a dilapidated shack with a corrugated iron roof. It was home to an unshaven young monk in gray cotton shirt and trousers. His face lit up on seeing us. He disappeared into his smoky kitchen to make tea.

Eight hundred years earlier, in 1205, Korean Zen master Chinul spent the autumn in retreat at Baekun Am. One day a monk called Hyesim came to visit him. While "resting at the foot of the mountain, still more than a thousand steps from the hermitage," Hyesim heard Chinul call out to his attendant for tea, which prompted him to write this verse:

> I hear a call to a boy
> echoing through misty pines,
> the aroma of steeping tea
> wafts down this stony path.

On reaching the hermitage, Hyesim recited the poem to Chinul. Chinul laughed and gave Hyesim the fan he was holding. Hyesim uttered the lines:

> On meeting fiery haste
> and crazy deeds—
> it's a good idea
> to cool them down.

Five years later Chinul died. At the age of thirty-two, Hyesim was ordered by royal decree to lead the "Prajñā and Samādhi Community" Chinul had founded at what is today the monastery of Songgwang Sa.

In my late twenties, I spent nearly four years at Songgwang Sa, training as a Zen monk under the guidance of Kusan Sunim. For three months each summer and three months each winter, I would meditate ten hours each day. The first session began at 3 AM, the last ended at 9 PM. Each hour involved fifty minutes sitting cross-legged on a cushion and ten minutes walking briskly round the hall. The only sounds were the mechanical ticking of a hand-wound clock on one wall and the periodic *clack!* of a wooden *djukpi* struck by the practice leader.

On opening my eyes, I would see a patch of waxed yellow-ochre paper covering the floor on which I sat and a bare white wall in front of me. Since both the latticed doors and windows were pasted over with rice paper, I could not see outside. About ten monks sat in the hall each season, but I had rarely been so completely alone.

All I had to do was ask: "What is this?" My mind soon grew weary of the ingenious answers it conjured up. Posing the question was more interesting than finding a solution. As I probed and explored the raw fact of being alive, my accumulated opinions about life and its meaning fell away. I came to rest in a calm expanse of puzzlement and ignorance. Questioning and not-knowing ceased to be anything exceptional. They seeped into my flesh and bones; they enlivened my senses.

At Baekun Am, I sipped my tea from a chipped porcelain cup. I had not been back to Korea for twenty-eight years. I had put on weight and what was left of my hair had turned white. None of my Korean friends recognized me. I was none the wiser about what "this" is. I was more perplexed than ever.

This pilgrimage honored the thirtieth anniversary of Kusan Sunim's death in 1983. Led by his Korean disciple Hyonho, we were traveling by bus to the places where our teacher had meditated, worked, and taught. Like Chinul, Kusan had also spent time in retreat at Baekun Am. Just as Hyesim had first met Chinul here, so too had Hyonho first met Kusan. As the days passed, it became clear that we had not trekked up this remote mountain merely to contemplate the benefits of solitude.

The monastery was preparing for another succession. After Kusan died, Ilgak Sunim became the Zen master. After Ilgak died, Posong Sunim succeeded him. Now old and infirm, Posong would not be able to fulfil his duties much longer. As the time for succession approaches, the senior members of the monastic "family" discreetly maneuver themselves into a favorable position to be selected for the post.

A crew from the Buddhist Television Network accompanied us wherever we went. A two-part documentary was being made on the pilgrimage, prominently featuring us Westerners and a Sri Lankan. Cameraman Mr. Jang and sound technician Mr. Kim filmed our arduous ascent up to Baekun Am. Against the backdrop of forest, rock, and sky, each foreigner was invited to share with the camera his or her impressions of the hermitage and recollections of Kusan.

Solitude is converted into religious capital. Withdrawal from the affairs of the world becomes a political asset. The hardship of renunciation generates revenue, power, and renown. Meditating for months on end in a Zen hall is well and good, but enlightenment is inseparably linked in the Korean mind with solitary practice in places like Baekun Am. After resigning as head of monastic affairs in Cholla Namdo province, Kusan Sunim spent three years here, which culminated in an awakening that he recorded in verse:

Penetrating deep into a pore of Samantabhadra,
Mañjuśrī is seized and defeated.
Now the great earth is quiet.
It is hot on the day of the winter equinox;
Pine trees are of themselves green.
A stone man, riding a crane, flies over the blue mountains.

26

Aldous Huxley died in California on November 22, 1963, oblivious to what had happened earlier that day in Dallas. Fifty minutes after a bullet tore through John F. Kennedy's brain, Huxley's wife, Laura, injected her dying husband with one hundred micrograms of LSD. He passed away serenely six hours later.

Huxley's exploration of psychedelics began one sunny May morning in 1953, when he drank half a glass of water containing four-tenths of a gram of mescaline, the psychoactive alkaloid of the peyote cactus. His essay "The Doors of Perception" offers an impassioned, meandering account of what happened next. Huxley describes taking the medicine, then says:

> We live together, we act on, and react to, one another; but always and in all circumstances we are by ourselves. The martyrs go hand in hand into the arena; they are crucified alone. Embraced, the lovers desperately try to

fuse their insulated ecstasies into a single self-transcendence; in vain. By its very nature every embodied spirit is doomed to suffer and enjoy in solitude.

While acknowledging this existential aloneness, Huxley was also convinced that disciplined meditation or the ingestion of the right chemical would let him "know from the inside" what visionaries, artists, and mystics throughout history had reported.

In taking mescaline Huxley hoped to break free of the confinements of his neurotic ego and experience directly the wisdom that constitutes the "perennial philosophy," which, in his 1946 book of the same name, he defined as

> a metaphysic that recognizes a divine Reality substantial to the world of things and lives and minds; the psychology that finds in the soul something similar to, or even identical with, divine Reality; the ethic that places man's final end in the knowledge of the immanent and transcendent Ground of all being.

Huxley was not disappointed. He recounts beholding "what Adam had seen on the morning of creation—the miracle, moment by moment, of naked existence." He found that mescaline, in the language of the poet and artist William Blake, "cleansed the doors of perception," allowing everything to "appear to man as it is, infinite." Like others before him, he was dumbstruck by the utter incapacity of reason and language to make sense of the paradox of existence: "a transience that is yet eternal life, a perpetual perishing that is at the same time pure Being."

Asked by a friend to describe what he was seeing, he replied: "The nearest approach to this would be a Vermeer." For Huxley, this "mysterious artist" captured better than any other the sublime givenness of ordinary things. Vermeer possessed the rare gift, he says, to behold "the Dharma-Body of the Buddha as the hedge at the bottom of the garden." Until he took mescaline, Huxley had considered this Zen kōan a "vaguely pregnant piece of nonsense." Now, he said, "it was all as clear as day, as evident as Euclid."

Vermeer succeeds in arresting life in its pivotal moments while losing nothing of its vitality and generosity. The simplest things— a nail in a wall, metal studs on a chair, a plain white curtain in shadow, a trickle of water down an alley—appear suffused with unworldly intensity and significance. His darkest, most saturated colors radiate luminosity. For Huxley, Vermeer reveals the "divine, essential Not-self" of inanimate objects. The glass pane in Vermeer's door of perception that opens onto things, Huxley says, is "perfectly transparent." The pane that opens onto human beings, however, is "still muddy." For although Vermeer represented people, Huxley maintains that he was always "a painter of still life."

To capture the essential Not-self of people, Huxley implies that Vermeer had to paint them as objects: "in repose, their minds untroubled, their bodies motionless." Vermeer sought to portray the young women in his paintings as "girls to the very limit," provided they "refrain from behaving girlishly." Only in these circumstances could he "see Suchness in all its heavenly beauty." For in contrast to these works of Vermeer there stands, for Huxley, "the all-inclusive art of Rembrandt," an art that displays humanity in all its conceited, ambiguous tragedy.

Despite impeccable secular credentials as grandson of T. H. Huxley, the biologist known as "Darwin's Bulldog," Aldous Huxley was a theist. His perennial philosophy enabled him to consider the Dharma-Body of the Buddha as just another way of talking about the Godhead. Mescaline, he believed, had opened his eyes to the "Mind at Large," which the survival-driven "reducing valve" of petty human consciousness blocks out. Everything Huxley says in "The Doors of Perception" is filtered through the lens of this mystical universalism.

My own journeys with peyote and ayahuasca have left intact my long-standing agnostic, skeptical, and middle-way perspective on life. Just as mescaline confirmed Huxley's philosophical outlook, so peyote and ayahuasca have intensified and deepened mine. Such substances may have temporarily switched off Huxley's "reducing valve"—which today neuroscientists might call the brain's "default-mode network"—but that's all. There is no need to evoke the Godhead or a "Mind at Large" to account for what happens under the influence of psychedelics. Huxley's language suggests an embedded bias toward theistic ways of conceiving of the self and world. Rather than cherish an open, endlessly curious mind, he reaches for a religious or metaphysical explanation. When the default-mode network is suspended, whether through meditation or medicine, one encounters life with speechless, primordial wonder. And that is more than enough.

I first read "The Doors of Perception" when I was seventeen or eighteen years old. Huxley's journey overlapped with my own life; he had ingested those four-tenths of a gram of mescaline one month after I was born. But I did not read the essay again until shortly after I had completed the first draft of *The Art of Solitude* and the book had been accepted for publication. One evening I was seized by an impulse to look at "The Doors of Perception" once more. I downloaded it onto my iPad. Only then did I rediscover that Huxley had framed his experience of mescaline with the idea of solitude, explained its effects in the language of Buddhism, and compared what he was seeing to the paintings of Vermeer. Did I already know this? Had those associations been imprinted in my adolescent brain? Did buried memories inform the writing of this book all along? I have no idea.

27

He who loves teachings

that are biased, contrived, and obscure,

seeing only his own advantage,

rests on a peace with shaky foundations.

FOUR EIGHTS, 2:5

"There is a plague on man," says Montaigne: "the opinion that he knows something." As a Christian, Montaigne believed that this sickness began in the Garden of Eden, when the Devil first "insinuated himself within us with promises of knowledge and understanding." The philosophical practice of solitude enables man in his fallen state to experience untroubledness (*ataraxia*) akin to the natural simplicity and innocence of Eden. But there is a higher, mystical solitude that leads to God. "The idea of those who seek solitude out of devotion," says Montaigne, "inspired by the certainty of God's promises for the life to come, is much more sane and appropriate." Montaigne saw himself as a philosopher and Christian, but not as a mystic. He could only admire those whose souls were "ablaze with vital faith and hope," since they "construct in their solitude a life of delight and rapture far beyond any other kind of life."

Pyrrhonism may reveal man "naked, empty, and aware of his natural weakness" but that is not enough. Ataraxia can become a stepping-stone to something greater. "Stripped of human knowledge," Montaigne explains,

> man is all the more suited for the divine to dwell within him. Annihilating his intellect in order to make more room for faith, he is suited to receive mysterious powers from on high. . . . He is freed from the vain and irreligious opinions introduced by false sects. He is a blank sheet, ready for the finger of God to inscribe on him whatever it pleases.

Montaigne turns the philosophy of Pyrrho into a weapon in the wars of religion. Its role in this battle is to "wrench from our grasp the puny weapons of our reason, to make us lower our heads and bite the earth in reverence before the authority of divine majesty." For "whoever sees man without flattery will see in him no gifts or faculties that smell of anything other than death and dust. The more we grant, owe, and render to God, the more Christianly we act." That is why "ignorance is advocated so much by our religion as a quality suited to belief and obedience."

The philosophers of ancient Athens and Rome scaled the heights of human wisdom but failed even to scratch the surface of reality. "Truth is not, as Democritus said, hidden deep down in abysses," Montaigne remarks, "but raised to an infinite height within divine understanding." Even "the virtuous actions of Socrates and of Cato remain vain and useless, since they did not have, as their end or their aim, love of the true Creator of all things or obedience to him: they did not know God." In advocating a life free from opinions, skepticism is a philosophy that readies us for the revelation of the Gospels.

Montaigne accepts that the "infinite jurisdiction" of God, which mysteriously orders the unfolding of the universe, is revealed through the Roman Catholic Church and its representative on earth, the pope. The authority of monarchs and the social order based upon it stem from the king's sanctification by the church. Our laws on earth are thus vouchsafed by God. Montaigne might deplore the treatment of the indigenous peoples of the Americas, but he accepts it as part of a divine plan that he is incapable of understanding. "The Christian religion," he says, "bears all the hallmarks of supreme justice and utility, but none is more clear than the specific injunction to obey the authorities and uphold the political system." "Since I am incapable of choosing," he admits,

> I accept another's choice and remain where God has placed me. Otherwise, I would not know how to prevent myself from endlessly spinning in circles. By God's grace I have kept myself whole, without agitation or a troubled conscience, within the ancient beliefs of our religion amid all the many sects and schisms that our century has produced.

For Montaigne, it is not the church that needs to be reformed but our vain and presumptuous selves. This inner reformation takes place in our solitude.

> Within himself the wise man should withdraw his soul from the crowd, maintaining its power to judge things freely. As for what is outside, he should strictly follow all received forms and customs.

Pyrrhonists, too, recognize that since we cannot trust either our senses or reason, we need to be guided in our behavior by the customs and traditions of our time and place. "Laws remain effective," says Montaigne, "not because they are just but because they are laws. This is the mystical basis of their authority. They have no other."

It is therefore "highly doubtful whether any obvious benefit can come from changing an established law, whatever it may be, compared with the evil of contesting it." "I am disgusted by novelty," says Montaigne in reference to the Reformation, "and am right to be so, for I have seen some of its disastrous effects."

> To speak frankly, there seems to be great self-love and presumption in granting your opinions such esteem that you can justify disrupting the public peace in order to establish them.

"Nothing undermines the State like innovation," he concludes. "Change by itself creates injustice and tyranny."

The sheer arrogance of the Protestant reformers astounds him:

> How delusional seem the ideas of those who, in recent years, have the habit of accusing any bright, clearheaded person who professes the Catholic religion of only pretending to do so. To show him respect, they even maintain that despite what he appears to say, deep inside he cannot fail to have "reformed" beliefs just like them. What a deplorable sickness to be so convinced of being right that you persuade yourself that nobody could believe otherwise.

In the end, Montaigne fails to get the job in Rome. His friend Paul de Foix, the archbishop of Toulouse, is appointed French ambassador to the Vatican instead. As a consolation prize Montaigne is granted a "Bull of Roman Citizenship, resplendent with seals and gilded letters" and a request from King Henry III for him to become mayor of Bordeaux. The papal authorities find nothing objectionable in the *Essays* apart from the occasional use of profane language and a curious devotion to Fortune. It is left to Montaigne's own discretion to make any changes. He makes none. His philosophy of radical ignorance and unconditional faith poses no difficulties for the church—as he well would have known.

Montaigne heads slowly back to Bordeaux, lingering at spas and shrines on the way. "On arriving there," he recalls, "I presented my character faithfully and truly, exactly as I know it to be: no memory, no vigilance, no experience, no drive; no hatred either, no ambition, no desire, no violence—so that they should be well informed about what to expect from my service." After two unremarkable terms as mayor, he comments: "They also say that my period of office passed without mark or trace. Good."

Montaigne now retires to his tower, where he writes what will be the third and final volume of the *Essays*. He continues in private to maintain contact with the key figures of both the Protestant and Catholic camps in the civil war. The Protestant king Henry of Navarre, a man he greatly admires, is twice a guest at his estate. In 1584, the year of his first visit to Montaigne, Henry becomes heir to the French throne on the death of the younger brother of the childless Henry III. When Henry III is assassinated by a religious fanatic five years later in 1589, Henry of Navarre automatically becomes King Henry IV of France, despite the strong objections by Catholics who cannot accept the notion of a Protestant king.

Montaigne dies in 1592 at the age of fifty-nine during a Mass held in his bedchamber. The following year, Henry of Navarre solemnly abjures the Protestant faith and returns to Catholicism, which allows him to be consecrated as king of France in Chartres cathedral in 1594. Four years later, the "good king Henry" issues the Edict of Nantes, which guarantees tolerance to Protestants and finally brings the wars of religion to an end. Had Montaigne lived to witness these events, he would no doubt have been gratified by the triumph of Catholicism and the role he may have played in nudging Henry back into the papal fold.

In 1595, Montaigne's adoptive daughter, Marie de Gournay, publishes the definitive (Bordeaux) edition of the *Essays*. For the rest of her life she devotes herself to promoting Montaigne's legacy, overseeing eleven posthumous editions of the *Essays* before her own death in 1645. The Roman Catholic Church places the *Essays* on the *Index of Prohibited Books* in 1676, where they remain until the *Index* is abolished in 1966. No official reason is given for this prohibition, but it seems that the authorities objected to Montaigne's fideism: the heretical view that faith and reason are incompatible, and that salvation is attained through faith alone.

28

After walking many miles, the woman comes to the bank of a wide river. There is no bridge or boat in sight, just a vast expanse of water. She cannot swim. There is no one around to help her. She cannot return to where she came from. She is completely alone.

She gathers together a few dead branches scattered on the ground, pulls out some reeds by the riverbank, and sets about building a raft. Once the raft is assembled, she pushes it into the water, wades out after it, lies down on it, and starts paddling with her hands and feet. By the time she gets to the far bank the raft is breaking apart and partially submerged. She clambers ashore. Then she continues on her way.

This is the story of a migrant or refugee in search of a better life. She needs courage to sever her ties to her family, her clan, her village, everything she has known and loved since childhood. It is terrifying to be so alone, but she has no choice. This is her first real experience of solitude.

Gotama lived at a time when a vast patchwork of small-scale agrarian communities was giving way to the emergence of the first monarchies and cities in northeast India. The economic surplus produced by farming the rich alluvial soil of the Gangetic basin enabled kings to establish standing armies, build fortified cities, and mint coins, while ordinary people could leave home to become merchants, soldiers, monks, and philosophers. All were united in their experience of breaking with the past in order to pursue new opportunities. After generations of living in tight-knit village communities where little changed and everyone was secure in their role and relationships, suddenly you had to confront being alone in the world.

Whether you were a nun, a trader, or a minister, the dharma provided you with the contemplative skills needed to manage this newfound solitude. By cultivating mindfulness and collectedness, you steadied your attention, established a source of inner well-being, and became more focused and autonomous. You were encouraged to fully embrace each new situation, let go of your fears and reactive emotions, ground yourself in the nonreactive space of nirvana, and then choose a way of life that enabled you to flourish as a person. By activating imagination and creativity, whoever embarked on this path was said to become "independent of others."

Gotama used the parable of the raft to illustrate that the middle way he teaches is provisional. The dharma is a means to an end, not an end in itself. It serves "the purpose of crossing over, not the purpose of grasping." It may help you resolve certain conflicts, but once that is done, you should leave it behind and get on with your life. To treat the dharma as an end would be like hoisting the sodden raft onto your shoulders and lugging it with you. What once saved your life would be turned into a burden that hinders your progress.

When his followers had mastered the basic training skills, Gotama told them to "go forth into the world for the welfare of the many, and let no two of you follow the same path." Communal living was temporary and provisional too. It was also like a raft. Gathering in a grove or park during the monsoon provided you with a valuable framework for learning, but as soon as the rains were over, the community disbanded. Your responsibility lay in the world: not just in helping others live more autonomously, but in serving as an embodiment of solitary self-sufficiency.

Some five hundred years after Gotama and his first disciples walked the plains of northern India, the Buddhist philosopher Nāgārjuna wrote:

> When buddhas don't appear
> And their followers are gone,
> The wisdom of awakening
> Bursts forth by itself.

Nāgārjuna refers to "solitary buddhas," people who awaken to nirvana and the middle way through their own inquiry, quite independent of Buddhism. The dharma is a law or way of life that is intuitively "sensed by the wise," irrespective of whether you be Buddhist, Christian, Muslim, atheist, or agnostic. It may never occur to such accidental buddhas to become teachers, formulate doctrines, or found communities. As masters of the art of solitude they spontaneously lead their lives from the standpoint of nirvana.

The English poet John Keats knew nothing about Buddhism, but his concept of "negative capability" captures the nirvanic perspective as well as any Buddhist definition. This negative capability is present whenever one

> is capable of being in uncertainties, mysteries, doubts, without any irritable reaching after fact and reason.

For Keats, this quality of mind was most apparent in an artist such as Shakespeare, whom he considered "the least of an egoist that it was possible to be. He was nothing in himself; but he was all that others were, or that they could become."

Nirvana is a negative capability. In letting go of—"negating"—reactivity, one discovers a greater capacity—"capability"—to respond to life. To experience nirvana is to experience freedom from those attachments and opinions that prevent your own imaginative response to the situations you face in life. Nirvana is not the end point of the path but its turning point.

In the second century BCE, the Buddhist monk Nāgasena explained to the Indo-Greek king Menander how Gotama had designed, laid out, and built the City of Nirvana. Unlike a modern city with its endless suburban sprawl, the city of nirvana is a walled city, an enclosed civic space governed by the rule of law. Such was the destination of those who left home and crossed rivers on rafts in search of a better life. The walled city arising from the Gangetic plain came to serve as a metaphor for the "inner citadel" of one's own solitude, which, framed by the law of dharma, enables negative capability.

29

He doesn't elaborate, nor does he flatter—

he has not taken up any teachings.

You cannot gauge this priest by his rules,

he has gone beyond—with nothing to fall back on.

FOUR EIGHTS, 4:8

If I cross the Dordogne at Branne, it takes forty minutes to drive to Saint-Michel-de-Montaigne from where I live in the Entre-Deux-Mers. I arrive at the château at half past nine on a cold, misty December morning. The current owners have kindly allowed me to spend a morning alone in Montaigne's tower. On approaching the weathered wooden door of the tower, I am physically aware of the peculiar mix of anticipations and worries I feel. I realize that Montaigne did not just retire to the solitude of his tower;

he did so in a different mood and frame of mind each time he entered it.

I unroll my meditation mat and place it in the center of the circular chapel on the ground floor. As my eyes grow used to the light from the single window, I can see the altar recessed in one wall, two high-backed prayer stools placed before it. Above and behind me to the left I can just make out the stepped listening channel—formerly part of a narrow stairway—that Montaigne had preserved so that when bedridden upstairs he could hear the priest intone the mass. Settling into meditation, I am absorbed in the chapel's audible ambient hush. I chant the syllables OM MANI PADME HUM and listen to the words echo and linger around me.

With the château shuttered up for the winter, its courtyard locked and deserted, and no tour groups scheduled that day, it is much quieter than it would have been in Montaigne's time, with the constant hubbub of a self-sufficient community of bakers, blacksmiths, servants, cooks, woodcutters, farmers, and children in the courtyard. Today, the silence of the chapel is penetrated only by the remote noise of a tractor as it performs an unknown task somewhere in the vineyards outside. Then I hear a distant church bell ring ten times to mark the hour.

I climb the circular staircase, each step worn away unevenly. I pause in the living quarters on the first floor, where Montaigne died. I notice the primitive toilet: an extrusion from the wall of the staircase with a hole—now filled—in the floor. Finally, I reach the library on the second floor, where Montaigne spent "most days of my life and most hours of each day" reading books and composing essays. I open the shutters of the three small windows and the room is suffused with the gray light of late autumn. Étienne de la Boétie's and Montaigne's books are long gone. The space is bare except for a plaster statue of Montaigne, a table with a photocopy of a page from the Bordeaux edition of the *Essays,* a chair, and two disintegrating saddles. The roof beams above still bear the Latin and Greek quotations that inspired him.

I lay out my meditation mat and sit down cross-legged in the middle of the room, facing where the bookcases would have stood. I take out my iPad and spend the rest of the morning organizing and editing my selection of Montaigne's thoughts on solitude. Again I admire his limpid and ruthlessly honest prose. "Cut these words," said Ralph Waldo Emerson, "and they would bleed; they are vascular and alive." At times I close my eyes and sit still in the lifeless silence of the place. I ponder the small terra-cotta bricks, some now chipped and cracked, of which the floor is made, imagining Montaigne's feet on them as he paces round the room. When the church bell rings for noon, my fingers are numb with cold.

The prospect of being able to spend a morning alone in Montaigne's tower was thrilling. The reality was much the same as if I had sat by myself in any other unheated, poorly lit, and slightly dilapidated medieval building. But now I know what it feels like to be alone in the tower. Unlike my previous experiences of being herded through the building in a tour group, I now have tasted what it is like to pray in the chapel and write in the library. The tower has assumed more solemn and intimate contours.

On leaving the tower, I walk through the grounds of the estate to the village church of Saint-Michel-de-Montaigne. After being burned down during the wars of religion, it was rebuilt by funds provided by Montaigne's widow, Françoise de la Cassaigne. As I leave the village, the sun breaks through the mist. I pass row after row of bare vines, interrupted by woodlands of oak and chestnut still ablaze with golden leaves. I walk past farmsteads and fallow fields until I reach the church of Saint-Pierre-ès-Liens in the small town of Montcaret.

Originally connected to a twelfth-century Benedictine monastery, Saint-Pierre was razed to the ground during the battle to reclaim it for the Catholic Church at the outbreak of the wars of religion. It was not fully reconstructed for another three hundred years. In 1873 the local priest noticed that some of the soil being taken from a disused part of the cemetery for the construction of a railway station contained pieces of masonry. This and further finds led to archaeological excavations, which revealed the presence of an extensive fourth-century CE Roman villa beneath the church and the cemetery.

The church of Saint-Pierre was built on top of and in part from the remains of this pagan villa. Montaigne had marveled at Seneca's descriptions of houses heated with hypocaust systems that circulated hot air beneath the floors and through the walls. Were he alive now, he could view such a system for himself only three miles from his tower. The Visitors' Center at the site is dominated by the villa's restored dining room, tastefully enclosed in a minimalist steel, pine, and glass structure. Leisured men in togas may once have reclined on couches here to discuss philosophy, even the "wisest philosophy" of them all: skepticism. In the Middle Ages, gravediggers inadvertently dug through the floor of this room. The skeletons of three Christian souls still lie here in their rough cavities amid an expanse of patterned Gallo-Roman mosaic.

30

I do not regard myself as a particularly accomplished meditator. I know others who appear far more dedicated to meditation than I am. Had I been more serious, surely I would have committed far more time to the jhānas than two weeklong retreats. Yet despite my interest in this practice, I have little inclination to spend weeks or months further refining or deepening it. One reason for this lack of interest is that I still notice, many months later, how the effects of these jhāna retreats continue to influence my attention and awareness not only in formal meditation but in everyday life. Collectedness (*samādhi*) has now become more integral to my daily practice. My meditation has become more embodied and I give greater value to contentment, rapture, and well-being as part of the process.

Jhāna practice has helped me understand that the traditional Buddhist distinction between "stillness" (*samatha*) and "insight" (*vipassanā*) can be misleading. While it might be necessary to present them as distinct practices at the outset, as one's meditation matures they become increasingly inseparable. In theory I knew this from my Buddhist studies. Yet it was only through doing these jhāna retreats that I understood what it meant in my own embodied experience.

Over the years I must have spent many thousands of hours seated on a meditation cushion, but I still get distracted, listless, and bored. On a typical retreat, I will have good days and bad days. I can sometimes be overwhelmed by an obsessive worry that plagues me for hours. My mood can swing between elation and despondency from one moment to the next. There can be long periods when I do not meditate formally at all. Often I feel like a dilettante.

So why do I persist in an activity that in many respects seems to have made little difference to what goes on in my own mind? I have learned that the value of meditation is not that it changes the content of your experience. It changes your relationship to that content. All the worries, egotistic fantasies, lusts, and pettiness that surge into consciousness are simply the result of previous conditions over which I have little control. They are naturalistic processes that happen independent of my volition. I do not choose to feel them. All I can do is be mindful of them as they arise, recognize them for what they are, and not let myself be too influenced or swept away by them.

In trying over the years to lead a mindful and ethical life, I may have reduced the conditions that provoke the most egregious forms of reactivity. By not acting on those reactions, I may not reinforce them as much now as I did in the past, thus lessening the frequency of their occurrence. Yet how can I know that such benefits are not simply the result of maturity or other factors that have nothing to do with formal meditation practice? Can I be sure that I wouldn't be experiencing the same thing now even if I had never sat a single hour cross-legged on a cushion? Scientific studies into the effects of meditation are seeking to answer these questions. While some of the findings suggest that meditation may indeed be a key factor in producing such changes, it would be premature at this point to draw sweeping conclusions about its effectiveness.

As the person in whom the effects of meditation unfold, I am probably in the worst position to judge them. I am too close to the process to be able to see with any clarity the consequences of a practice that I have been doing for so long. Rather than ask me, you should ask my wife, my brother, my old friends. I doubt their answers would be unambiguous.

In the end, the only thing that really matters for me as a meditator is how well or badly I respond to the challenges and opportunities presented by the situation at hand. If my contemplative practice fails to contribute to my flourishing as a person in my relationships with others, then I have to question the purpose of spending months and years practicing it. Every moment in life offers the chance to start afresh. I can embrace what is before me, let go of what holds me back, then speak or act in a way that is not determined by my fears, attachments, or egotistic conceits. Although I frequently fail in my attempts to live in this way, I am convinced that mindfulness, collectedness, and questioning are crucial to my ability to do so.

I likewise do not doubt that by training oneself in contemplative disciplines one can achieve nonordinary states of mind that might sound incredible for those unfamiliar with these things. When Leigh describes dwelling for long periods of time in the jhānas and immaterial absorptions, I have no reason to disbelieve him. fMRI scans of Leigh's brain in meditation have shown different areas lighting up as he enters different jhānic states. Yet I suspect that the ability to access such altered forms of consciousness is due to a range of factors other than formal training. Not only are some people more highly motivated to achieve such states, they may be more temperamentally and perhaps neurobiologically suited than others to enter them.

"We had the experience," wrote T. S. Eliot in "The Dry Salvages," "but missed the meaning." The meaning of contemplation must not be confused with the experience of contemplation. To be able to dwell in a deeply focused, ecstatic, and clear state of mind is in itself meaningless. You can train and develop your spiritual muscles to an exceptional degree without necessarily flourishing much as a person. Your meditation is meaningful to the extent that it contributes to your becoming the kind of person you aspire to be. And since an ethical vision is integral to your life as a whole, it will inform, suffuse, and transform your contemplative practice.

To integrate contemplative practice into life requires more than becoming proficient in techniques of meditation. It entails the cultivation and refinement of a sensibility about the totality of your existence—from intimate moments of personal anguish to the endless suffering of the world. This sensibility encompasses a range of skills: mindfulness, curiosity, understanding, collected-ness, compassion, equanimity, care. Each of these can be culti-vated and refined in solitude but has little value if it cannot survive the fraught encounter with others. Never be complacent about contemplative practice; it is always a work in progress. The world is here to surprise us. My most lasting insights have oc-curred off the cushion, not on it.

31

I pass the morning walking aimlessly through the narrow streets of the old city of Málaga. Along the boulevards, green parakeets flash and shriek between palm trees. The dazzling winter sun intensifies the mild headache I attribute to not having drunk coffee for three days. I feel faintly nauseous, which I connect to a bowl of unheated pasta I ate last night in Lisbon. I am tired and tense; my joints ache as if I might come down with the flu. I have not eaten today. I have drunk only orange juice and tea.

I worry about my motives for taking ayahuasca. It has been a year since I attended the ceremony with Salvador. I still feel the need to explore this medicine further. Four months ago, my friend Michael Stone—a charismatic yoga and meditation teacher, author, and political activist—died from an overdose of the synthetic opioid fentanyl. His wife was expecting their third child. In a statement, the family revealed that Michael was suffering from increasingly severe bipolar disorder, which he had concealed from his friends and students. The fentanyl was probably an attempt to control his mania. I worry whether my liberal attitude toward psychoactive substances might have contributed to the tolerant culture that tacitly gave him permission to experiment with an illegal opioid more potent than heroin. What Michael needed from a Buddhist teacher like myself may have been an unambiguous example to abstain from all such substances.

A Mercedes taxi drives me east out of Málaga into the olive groves and pine-dashed hills of Andalucía. One hour later, we leave the village of San Juan and bump down a narrow valley road until we reach a farmstead, its orchard abundant with oranges, lemons, persimmons, and pomegranates. I place my blankets, cushion, shawl, and water bottle on the heated stone floor of the plain white hall where the ceremony will be held. I know none of the other thirteen participants, nor Hemming, the shaman.

It is a new moon. The hall flickers with the light of a single candle and a log fire in an iron grate in one corner. We sit in a semicircle. Hemming, a self-effacing Dane in his late forties, is seated on a low chair before us. We meditate for twenty minutes, settling into the collective silence that will last until dawn. Hemming puffs on a cigarette and blows the smoke into a plastic bottle of ayahuasca. We take it in turns to receive a dose of the medicine in a small glass. I drink it in one gulp. It has that same deeply familiar and repellent taste I struggle to identify but cannot.

I sit cross-legged but shift about uncomfortably. Within what seems like a few minutes, my body prickles with heat. I pull a plastic bucket toward me and am violently sick. I briefly worry that I will disgorge the medicine before it has time to take effect. I cannot stop retching. My mind is invaded by spiraling patterns of color. I vomit diminishing amounts of a bitter liquid, my body repeatedly convulsing, sweat dripping off my face, my nostrils filled with the vegetal stench of the medicine, until I pass out.

Hemming kneels beside me, stroking my face with a wet condor feather. "Stephen," he whispers, "we are in the ceremony." I do not know how long I was unconscious. I am exhausted. I lie immobile on my back. I cannot consider standing up, let alone walking about. Even sitting is an effort. I want what has invaded my body to stop but can do nothing about it. This is unpleasant, but I am not anxious or troubled. I say to myself: I cannot drink another cup of this swamp juice tomorrow.

Over time my mind settles into contemplation. My body still hurts but feels cleansed by the purging. The nausea, headache, and flulike symptoms have gone. I sense that something entrenched within me has been dispelled but have no idea what it is. The medicine seems able to penetrate the darkest nooks and crannies to root out whatever still clings there.

I feel a confirmation again. It is as though the purging has forcibly opened and inscribed in my flesh a passageway for new possibilities to emerge. This purified space is nothing other than nirvana. The medicine lets you contemplate, feel, taste, and savor nirvana. The path of your life originates here. Nirvana is the uterus of the world. The very fabric of what I am is womblike, as if my thoughts and flesh are the matrix out of which I am born each moment. I rest in a still, ecstatic awareness, suffused with love for these intimate strangers who lie curled up on the floor around me in the darkness.

"You decide," I tell Hemming when he asks what dose I want the following night. He pours me half a glass, the same amount as before. I swallow the medicine. It no longer tastes so foul and sits more or less comfortably in my stomach. I neither vomit nor dry-heave.

As Mother Ayahuasca takes me in her arms, I realize that last night I vomited up my attachment to Buddhism. In passing out, I died. In coming to, I was, so to speak, reborn. *I no longer have to fight these battles,* I repeat to myself. *I am no longer a combatant in the dharma wars.* It feels as if the course of my life has shifted onto another vector, like a train shunted off its familiar track onto a new trajectory.

I tremble and shake, my arms and hands shudder, I moan and yawn uncontrollably. Hemming's assistant Bruno gently asks me to sit upright so I will make less noise. I have the impression of slipping into other realms, returning here, then slipping off again. This journey is like a roller-coaster ride through the chaotic field of stuff out of which we insatiably construe meaning.

At intervals Hemming sings *icaro,* medicine songs, his lone, affectless voice accompanied by the rattling of dried maize leaves. The spare pageant has something of the spectral, alien formality of Noh theater. I open my eyes to see a silhouetted figure kneeling beside me, an orange point of fire in the middle of its face. The spot of orange glows, then Hemming blows puffs of tobacco smoke over me and presses his palm on my heart. Without a face, Hemming becomes the wizened shaman animating these ceremonies outside ordinary time and place.

I keep coming back to the book I am writing, *The Art of Solitude*. I explore alternative words, rephrase sentences, experiment with chapter structure. I am aware that my thoughts about this book as I lie here on this warm floor become part of the book as soon as I think them. Is what is happening here already determined by the inner logic of my text? Is it colored by my knowledge that I will write about it? It is as though I am gazing into a mirror that reflects another mirror to behold an infinity of reflections. My life and my work have become so entangled I can barely tease them apart.

Ayahuasca may have done its work for me. My stomach rises to my gorge at the thought of drinking it again. I remind myself that the effectiveness of any medicine lies in reaching a point where you can stop taking it. If I still need to take it, then it has not yet cured me. And if the purpose of plant medicines is to open a closed heart, as Andrés said, then I need to measure their effectiveness by the openness of my heart—not just for the duration of a ceremony, which is easy, but when besieged by the conflicts and contradictions of ordinary life.

32

The Pali and Sanskrit word for "solitude" is *viveka.* It could also be translated as "separation," "isolation," or "seclusion." In Tibetan, *viveka* is *dben pa,* which the dictionary defines as the "absence" or "emptiness" of something. This is how Buddhists understand the term. Yet in Sanskrit Hindu texts *viveka* invariably means "discrimination," "distinction," "discernment," and "judgment." How did the same word come to assume different meanings in two Indian traditions that evolved side by side?

When you see a person in the distance, at first you may be able to judge only that it is a woman rather than a man. As she approaches, you start to make out that she is fair rather than dark, young rather than old. But she has to get much closer until you realize it is Mary rather than Jane. At each step you are able to discern certain features (female, fair, young) and eliminate others (male, dark, old) until you know it is

Mary. This process of discrimination is achieved by progressively isolating Mary from the wider perceptual field. You thereby make her stand out alone, distinct from everything she is not, a unique person existing in her own right.

Likewise, by withdrawing from the world into solitude, you separate yourself from others. By isolating yourself, you can see more clearly what distinguishes you from other people. Standing out in this way serves to affirm your existence (*ex*-[out] + *sistere* [stand]). Liberated from social pressures and constraints, solitude can help you understand better what kind of person you are and what your life is for. In this way you become independent of others. You find your own path, your own voice.

Gotama's final instruction to his community was this: "Be islands to yourselves. Let yourselves be your only refuge. Let the dharma be your island. Let the dharma be your only refuge." An island is a piece of dry land rising above yet surrounded by water. It is both isolated and insulated. The values and practices of the dharma that have been integrated into your life create a refuge from turmoil, a solitude where you can dwell in nonreactive emptiness of mind. This solitude is nirvana itself: a lucid space of freedom where you can respond to the world without being flooded by reactive desires, fears, hatreds, and opinions.

Emil Cioran once performed a thought experiment: "I suppressed word after word from my vocabulary," he explains. "When the massacre was over, only one had escaped: *solitude.* I awakened euphoric." Then it dawned on him: "the sole means of protecting your solitude is to offend everyone, beginning with those you love." Śāntideva pushes this reasoning further. For him, the solitary person has to die to the world. "Befriending no one, begrudging no one," he writes, "my body dwells in solitude: I am already counted as a dead man. No mourners will be at my grave."

Then something strange happens: as soon as he settles into his hard-won solitude, Śāntideva's attention returns to the very world he has been at pains to renounce. Only when his mind has quietened does he see that there is nothing special about himself at all. He is not essentially different from anyone else. Like the poet John Donne he understands that "no man is an island." He experiences all living beings, including himself, as symbiotic cells in a giant organism. "I should dispel the misery of others," he reflects, "because it is pain, just like my own, and I should help them, because they are sentient creatures, just like me." These are not the abstract conclusions of a moral philosopher. "When I live in this way," he continues, "no conceit arises. It is like feeding myself; I hope for nothing in return."

Here lies the paradox of solitude. Look long and hard enough at yourself in isolation and suddenly you will see the rest of humanity staring back. Sustained aloneness brings you to a tipping point where the pendulum of life returns you to others. Ingmar Bergman would retreat to the island of Fårö to plan his films and write his screenplays. "Here, in my solitude," he noted in his daily journal, "I have the feeling that I contain too much humanity," which "oozes out of me like from a broken tube of toothpaste; it doesn't want to stay within the confines of my body."

In China, Korea, and Japan, the sequence of Zen ox-herding pictures portrays a man who follows the footprints of an ox (the undisciplined mind) into a forest, tracks down the beast, tames it, and at last comes to settle in the peace of solitude, where both man and ox can be forgotten. The struggle over, the struggler disappears into an *enzo:* an empty Zen circle. Then, in the final frame, we see the man "appearing in the marketplace to teach and transform." Reflecting on her decade alone on a mesa in New Mexico, Agnes Martin concluded: "I stayed up there for years and became as wise as a Chinese hermit. Then I decided it was not a natural human way of living, to be so isolated, so I came back down."

"No pleasure has any taste for me when not shared with another," reflected Montaigne, "no happy thought occurs to me without my being irritated at bringing it forth alone with no one to offer it to." Even for those who do not choose solitude but have it imposed on them, the lesson can be the same. "It is never my custom to use words lightly," remarked Nelson Mandela. "If twenty-seven years in prison have done anything to us, it was to use the silence of solitude to make us understand how precious words are and how real speech is in its impact on the way people live and die."

In the end, the task is not to choose between a life of solitude and a life of engagement, but to embrace both and learn how to find a healthy balance between them. In his essay "Self Reliance," Emerson wrote:

> It is easy in the world to live after the world's opinion, it is easy in solitude to live after our own; but the great man is he who in the midst of the crowd keeps with perfect sweetness the independence of solitude.

In a blog addressed to students, the primatologist Jane Goodall quotes this passage and agrees with Emerson: "It is so important," she explains, that we find the independence of solitude as we try to enact change. Instead of becoming overwhelmed and suffocated by constant interaction with others, it is essential that we step back and allow ourselves the necessary alone time to reflect on what we care about.

Central to John Keats's understanding of solitude is that it provides the silence in which to pursue a thoughtful inner dialogue undisturbed. In his sonnet "O Solitude," he describes leaving behind "the jumbled heap of murky buildings" and retreating to hills "where the deer's swift leap startles the wild bee from the foxglove bell." As much as the poet enjoys such rural seclusion, he recognizes how his most soulful delight lies in

> the sweet converse of an innocent mind,
> Whose words are images of thoughts refin'd.

Here in this contemplative reverie—as concepts crystallize into imagery and circular inner monologue switches into dialogue between "two kindred spirits"—is true solitude realized.

*the four eight-verse poems from the aṭṭhakavagga
of the sutta nipāta*

Aṭṭhakavagga means "Chapter of Eights," the fourth of the five chapters (*vagga*) that make up the *Sutta Nipāta*, a collection of 1,149 verses, which is found in the *Khuddaka Nikāya* of the Pali Canon. The *Aṭṭhakavagga* itself consists of 209 verses, divided into sixteen sections, each of which is called a *sutta* (discourse). The four suttas I have translated here are titled:

- *Guhaṭṭhakasutta (The Discourse of Eight on the Cell)*
- *Duṭṭhaṭṭaksutta (The Discourse of Eight on Wrong)*
- *Suddhaṭṭakasutta (The Discourse of Eight on Purity)*
- *Paramaṭṭakasutta (The Discourse of Eight on the Ultimate)*

They make up the second, third, fourth, and fifth sections respectively of the *Aṭṭhakavagga,* and comprise verses 772–803 of the *Sutta Nipāta.*

In the notes to his 1992 translation of the *Sutta Nipāta*, K. R. Norman suggests:

Since the four *sutta*s which have *aṭṭhakasutta* in their names all have eight verses, in the Triṣṭubh metre, which is generally speaking an old metre in Pāli, we might reasonably suppose that these four *sutta*s are the core of the *Aṭṭhakavagga*, to which other *sutta*s have been added.

Furthermore, despite the chapter being called the *Chapter of Eights*, not a single one of its other twelve suttas has only eight verses—they contain between seven and twenty verses and also vary in meter.

If Mr. Norman's supposition is correct, then these four *sutta*s would have originally stood as an independent work of four eight-verse poems, which is how I treat them in my translation.

I also treat them as a literary work. I have insisted on the formal four-line structure of each verse and endeavored to find a voice that establishes a consistent rhythm and euphony. I have sought a wording that captures the disruptive spirit of the poems. As a result, my translation is freer than the other translations listed below.

The titles given to the suttas have been discarded, since they seem to be little more than convenient mnemonic devices drawn from words that occur in the first line of the first verse of the text but have no particular bearing on the theme of the individual sutta.

I followed the Pali Text Society edition of the *Sutta Nipāta* by Dines Andersen and Helmer Smith (1913, reprinted 1997). In addition, I consulted the English translations of H. Saddhatissa (1985), K. R. Norman (1992), Thanissaro Bhikkhu (1994–2013), John D. Ireland (1994–2013), and Gil Fronsdal (2016).

For a comprehensive study of the *Sutta Nipāta* and its commentarial tradition, see Bhikkhu Bodhi, trans., *The Suttanipāta: An Ancient Collection of the Buddha's Discourses Together with Its Commentaries* (Somerville, Mass.: Wisdom, 2017).

four eights

One

The creature concealed inside its cell—
a man sunk in dark passions
is a long, long way from solitude.
Hard is it to let go of what drives us,

hard to be free from the wants
that cleave to the thrill of being alive,
hankering for what's gone and to come,
hungering for those delights now—no one else can save you.

Obsessed, in dumb pursuit of pleasure,
you embark on a lonely, unbalanced life.
You cry out in anguish:
What will become of us when we leave here?

Be someone who practices right now.
Don't be thrown off course

for the sake of what you know to be unbalanced.
Life is short, declare the wise.

I see people tremble on this earth,
compelled by a thirst for what's going on—
weak men gabbling in the mouth of death,
their thirst for something and nothing unquenched.

You see them tremble for what's theirs,
like fish in shallow puddles of an arid gorge.
When you know this, act unselfishly—
form no attachment to what's happening.

Embrace what you meet and don't be obsessed—
subdue desire for both dead ends.
Avoid indulging in what you reproach yourself for—
the wise are not mired in views or words.

Embrace what you perceive and cross the flood.
The sage is untied to possessions—
having extracted the arrow, take care—
Don't long for this world or the next.

Two

Wrong-minded people voice opinions,
as do truth-minded people too.
When an opinion is offered, the sage is not drawn in—
there's nothing arid about the sage.

How can I, in thrall to longing,
self-satisfied and self-realized,
rise above my own point of view?
As I know myself, so I articulate myself.

The person, unsolicited,
who tells others of his morals
and offers opinions about himself—
the good declare to be ignoble.

Beggars at peace, completely at ease,
do not flaunt their virtues: *here I am!*
there's no one like me in the world—
the good opine that they are noble.

He who loves teachings
that are biased, contrived, and obscure,
seeing only his own advantage,
rests on a peace with shaky foundations.

You seize the teaching that suits those views
to which you're committed and cannot give up.
According to our commitments
do we reject or embrace a teaching.

Nowhere does a lucid one
hold contrived views about something or nothing.
How could he succumb to them,
having let go of illusions and conceit? He's uninvolved.

The involved get drawn into conflicting opinions about the dharma.
What opinion can you dispute with one who's uninvolved? And how?

He does not take up or discard any view—
he has shaken them all off, right here.

Three

I behold what is pure, supreme, unfailing
and am purified by this vision.
Convinced what you know is "ultimate,"
you believe your view is pure.

That a man be purified by visions,
his pain overcome by knowledge,
his attachments dispelled by others—
in stating these views, you betray an opinion.

Purity is nothing foreign,
says the priest not mired in views and words,
ideas and rules, good and evil.
He's discarded what he believed—and builds nothing here.

Dropping one, you clutch the next—
urged ahead by self-concern
you reject and adopt opinions
as a monkey lets go of a branch and seizes another.

You vow to practice alone
only to oscillate in the grip of perceptions.
The wise suffer no highs and lows—
having met the dharma through knowledge and learning.

One who takes no issue with things
sees what's before his eyes, is open to what is said,

acts in tune with what he senses.
Who can judge him here? By what measure?

He doesn't elaborate, nor does he flatter,
he is suspicious of "perfection"—
having cut the knots that bind,
he nurtures no longing for anything.

The priest without borders
doesn't seize on what he's known or beheld.
Not passionate, not dispassionate,
he doesn't posit anything as ultimate.

Four

One who dwells in "ultimate" views
and presents them as final
will declare all other views "inferior"—
he has not overcome disputes.

Seeing his own advantage
he seizes hold of views, words,
rules, and ideas in this way—
and sees everything else as base.

The good opine that he puts down others
because he has tied himself in knots.
The beggar does not get entangled
in views, words, ideas, or rules.

He does not elaborate a view
on the grounds of knowledge or morals—

he neither claims to be equal
nor thinks of himself as better or worse.

He lets go of one position without taking another—
he's not defined by what he knows.
Nor does he join a dissenting faction—
he assumes no view at all.

He's not lured into the blind alleys
of *something* and *nothing, this world* and *the next*—
for he lacks those commitments
that make people ponder and seize hold of teachings.

There's no hint of contrivance
in his perception of views, words and ideas—
who can judge the priest who holds no views?
By what standard can you measure him?

He doesn't elaborate, nor does he flatter—
he has not taken up any teachings.
You cannot gauge this priest by his rules,
he has gone beyond—with nothing to fall back on.

glossary

ATARAXIA (Greek). Literally, "untroubledness." Inner peace of mind. A key goal of Pyrrhonian and Epicurean philosophy.

AYAHUASCA (Quechua). A brew made from the *Banisteriopsis caapi* vine and leaves of the *Psychotria viridis* plant used in shamanic medicine ceremonies in Peru, Brazil, and elsewhere in South America.

BODHISATTVA (Sanskrit. Pali: *bodhisatta*). In early Buddhism, the epithet given to Gotama before his awakening. In Mahāyāna Buddhism, a person who aspires to awaken for the sake of others.

BUDDHA (Pali and Sanskrit). Literally: Awakened One. An epithet given to Gotama and others who have attained awakening.

CHACAPA (Quechua). A ritual leaf rattle used in shamanic medicine ceremonies.

DHARMA (Sanskrit. Pali: *dhamma*). Literally, "law." Dharma refers both to what Gotama awoke to and the teachings, values, and practices that lead to awakening.

DJUKPI (Korean). A stick of wood split down the middle used to make a clapping sound to mark the beginning and end of periods of Zen meditation.

ENZO (Japanese). A circle executed in a single brush stroke, symbolizing emptiness.

GOTAMA (Pali. Sanskrit: Gautama). A philosopher from the kingdom of Kosala in northeast India, known as the Buddha (c. 480–c. 400 BCE). His teachings form the basis of the Buddhist religion. A contemporary of Socrates.

ICARO (Quechua). Songs recited by a shaman during medicine ceremonies.

JHĀNA (Pali. Sanskrit: *dhyāna*). Literally, "meditation." In Buddhism it often refers to four phases of deepening collectedness, sometimes called "absorptions."

MAHĀYĀNA (Sanskrit). Literally, "Great Vehicle." A Buddhist reform movement that began about four hundred years after Gotama's death. The school of Buddhism that prevails in East and Central Asia.

MAÑJUŚRĪ (Sanskrit). In Mahāyāna Buddhism, the bodhisattva of wisdom.

MARA'AKAME (Huichol). An elder or shaman of the Huichol tribe in Mexico.

MESA (Spanish). Literally "table." A high plateau with a flat top and steep sides found in the American Southwest.

METATE (Spanish). A mealing stone for grinding grains.

OM MANI PADME HUM (Sanskrit). The mantra of Avalokiteśvara, the Mahāyāna bodhisattva of compassion.

NIRVANA (Sanskrit. Pali: *nibbāna*). The ending of greed, hatred, and confusion. Inner peace and freedom of mind. A key goal of Buddhist practice.

PALI (Pali). The mid-Indo-Aryan *prakrit* (spoken language) in which the teachings of Gotama were memorized and then written down.

PALI CANON. The five collections (*nikāya*) of teachings by Gotama and his disciples recorded in the Pali language.

PEYOTE (Spanish, derived from Aztec). *Lophophora williamsii.* A small spineless cactus used in shamanic medicine ceremonies in Mexico and elsewhere.

PRAJÑĀ (Sanskrit). Wisdom, understanding, discernment.

RAMPJAAR (Dutch). An *annus horribilis*, a terrible year.

SĀDHANĀ (Sanskrit). A ritual practice involving recitation, visualization, and meditation employed in tantric Buddhism.

SAMATHA (Pali and Sanskrit). Tranquility of mind realized through collectedness.

SAMĀDHI (Pali and Sanskrit). Collectedness of mind, concentration.

SAMANTABHADRA (Sanskrit). In Mahāyāna Buddhism, the bodhisattva who embodies fundamental goodness.

ŚĀNTIDEVA (Sanskrit). Eighth-century Mahāyāna Buddhist monk-poet, author of *A Guide to the Bodhisattva's Way of Life*.

SFUMATO (Italian). The technique in painting of allowing tones and colors to shade into one another, producing softened outlines.

SOJU (Korean). A distilled alcoholic beverage drunk in Korea.

STUPA (Sanskrit). Originally, a funerary mound; today, a domed architectural structure used throughout Asia as a symbol of the Buddha and the Dharma.

SUTTA (Pali). A discourse attributed to Gotama or one of his immediate disciples.

VAJRAYOGINĪ (Sanskrit). A female deity evoked in tantric Buddhist practices.

VIPASSANĀ (Pali. Sanskrit: *vipaśyanā*). Insight, or insight meditation.

VIVEKA (Pali and Sanskrit). Solitude.

YAMĀNTAKA (Sanskrit). A wrathful male deity evoked in tantric Buddhist practices.

ZEN (Japanese. Korean: *Sŏn*. Chinese: *Chan*). Literally: "meditation." The term is derived from the word *jhāna*. An East Asian Buddhist tradition that emphasizes disciplined contemplative practice as the way to awakening.

bibliography

Preamble

Batchelor, Stephen. *Alone with Others: An Existential Approach to Buddhism*. New York: Grove, 1983.

Catherine of Siena. *Letter (no. 49) to Monna Alessa dei Saracini*. http://www.drawnbylove.com/Scudder%20letters .htm#2MAlessa.

Fronsdal, Gil. *The Buddha before Buddhism: Wisdom from the Early Teachings*. Boulder, Colo.: Shambhala, 2016.

Hugo, Victor. *La fin de Satan*. 1886; Paris: Gallimard, 1984.

———. *Choses vues. Nouvelle série*. Paris: Calmann Lévy, 1900.

Wordsworth, William. *Selected Poems*. Ed. Stephen Gill. London: Penguin, 2004.

Art and Solitude
[YELLOW]
(Chapters 3, 7, 11, 14, 17, 21, 25, 32)

Auden, W. H. *Collected Poems*. Ed. Edward Mendelson. New York: Modern Library, 2007.

Avigdor, Leon d'. *Agnes Martin: Between the Lines*. Documentary film, 2016.

Batchelor, David. *Chromophobia*. London: Reaktion, 2000.

———. *The Luminous and the Grey*. London: Reaktion, 2014.

Buddhist Television Network. *Revering the Memory of Master Kusan Sunim 01*. Korean language video, available on YouTube. The section on Baekun Am starts at 11:04.

Buswell, Robert. *The Korean Approach to Zen: The Collected Works of Chinul*. Honolulu: University of Hawaii Press, 1983.

Cioran, E. M. *The Trouble with Being Born*. Trans. Richard Howard. London: Quartet, 1993.

Dehejia, Vidya. *Early Buddhist Rock Temples: A Chronological Study*. London: Thames and Hudson, 1972.

Emerson, Ralph Waldo. *Self Reliance and Other Essays*. 1841; New York: Dover, 1993.

Fergusson, James. *History of Indian and Eastern Architecture*. London: John Murray, 1910.

Gruen, John. " 'What We Make, Is What We Feel': Agnes Martin on Her Meditative Practice." 1976; *ARTnews,* 2015.

Hutchinson, John, et al. *Antony Gormley*. London: Phaidon, 1995, expanded ed. 2000.

Jelley, Jane. *Traces of Vermeer*. Oxford: Oxford University Press, 2017.

Keats, John. *Letters of John Keats*. Ed. Robert Gittings. Oxford: Oxford University Press, 1970.

Kull, Robert. *Solitude: Seeking Wisdom in Extremes*. Novato: New World Library, 2008. For photos and further information on Kull's solitude project, go to www.bobkull.org.

Lamotte, Étienne. *History of Indian Buddhism: From the Origins to the Śaka Era.* Trans. Sara Webb-Boin. Leuven: Peeters, 1988.

Maitland, Sara. *A Book of Silence.* London: Granta, 2008.

Martin, Agnes. *Writings/Schriften.* Ed. Dieter Schwarz. Ostfildern: Cantz-Verlag, 1993.

Martin, Henry. *Agnes Martin: Pioneer, Painter, Icon.* Tucson: Shaffner, 2018.

Mayer, Musa. *Night Studio: A Memoir of Philip Guston.* Munich: Sieveking Verlag, 1998.

Morris, Frances, and Tiffany Bell. *Agnes Martin.* Exhibition catalogue. New York: D.A.P/ Distributed Art Publishers, 2015.

Page, H. A. *Thomas de Quincey: His Life and Writings.* 2 Vols. London: 1877.

Princenthal, Nancy. *Agnes Martin: Her Life and Art.* New York: Thames and Hudson, 2015.

Śāntideva. *Śikshā-Samuccaya: A Compendium of Buddhist Doctrine.* Trans. Cecil Bendall and W. H. D. Rouse. 1922; Delhi: Motilal Banarsidass, 1971.

Schütz, Karl. *Vermeer: The Complete Works.* Cologne: Taschen GmbH, 2015.

Thoreau, Henry David. *Walden.* Ed. Jeffrey S. Cramer. 1854; New Haven: Yale University Press, 2004.

Van Dusen, Caitlin. "The Other Side of Appearance: An Interview with Antony Gormley." *Tricycle, the Buddhist Review,* Fall 2002.

Vermeer, Johannes. *A Maid Asleep* (1656–57), *The Milkmaid* (1658–61), *The Little Street* (1658–61), *Young Woman with a Water Pitcher* (1662–64), *Woman with a Lute* (1662–64), *Woman in Blue Reading a Letter* (1663–64), *Woman Holding a Balance* (1663–64), *Woman with a Pearl Necklace* (1663–64), *A Lady Writing* (1665–67), *The*

Lacemaker (1669–70), *The Art of Painting* (1666–68), *The Procuress* (1656). For details go to http://www.essentialvermeer.com.

Waiboer, Adriaan E., with Arthur K. Wheelock Jr. and Blaise Ducos. *Vermeer and the Masters of Genre Painting: Inspiration and Rivalry.* Exhibition catalogue. New Haven: Yale University Press, 2017.

Contemplation

[R E D]

(Chapters 1, 8, 12, 16, 20, 22, 28, 30)

Anālayo. *Satipaṭṭhāna: The Direct Path to Realization.* Cambridge: Windhorse, 2003.

Arbel, Keren. *Early Buddhist Meditation: The Four* Jhānas *as the Actualisation of Insight.* London: Routledge, 2016.

Batchelor, Stephen. *The Faith to Doubt: Glimpses of Buddhist Uncertainty.* 1990; Berkeley: Counterpoint, 2016.

———. *Verses from the Center: A Buddhist Vision of the Sublime.* New York: Riverhead, 2000.

Batchelor, Stephen, and Martine Batchelor. *What Is This? Ancient Questions for Modern Minds.* Wellington, N.Z.: Tuwhiri, 2019.

Bodhi, Bhikkhu, trans. *The Connected Discourses of the Buddha: A New Translation of the Saṃyutta Nikāya.* Somerville, Mass.: Wisdom, 2000.

Brasington, Leigh. *Right Concentration: A Practical Guide to the Jhānas.* Boston: Shambhala, 2015.

Eliot, T. S. *Collected Poems, 1909–1962.* London: Faber and Faber, 1963.

Hadot, Pierre. *The Inner Citadel: The Meditations of Marcus Aurelius.* Trans. Michael Chase. Cambridge: Harvard University Press, 1998.

Hart, William. *The Art of Living: Vipassanā Meditation: As Taught by S. N. Goenka*. London: HarperOne, 1987.

Horner, I. B., trans. *Milinda's Questions*. 2 vols. Bristol: Pali Text Society, 1963–64.

Kusan Sunim. *The Way of Korean Zen*. 1985; Boston: Weatherhill, 2009.

Ñāṇamoli, Bhikkhu, and Bhikkhu Bodhi, trans. *The Middle Length Discourses of the Buddha (Majjhima Nikāya)*. Boston: Wisdom, 1995.

Śāntideva. *A Guide to the Bodhisattva's Way of Life*. Trans. Stephen Batchelor. Dharamsala: LTWA, 1979.

Shankman, Richard. *The Experience of Samādhi: An In-depth Exploration of Buddhist Meditation*. Boston: Shambhala, 2008.

Siff, Jason. *Unlearning Meditation: What to Do when the Instructions Get in the Way*. Boston: Shambhala, 2010.

Walshe, Maurice, trans. *The Long Discourses of the Buddha: A Translation of the Dīgha Nikāya*. Boston: Wisdom, 1995.

Zangpo, Thogmé (Thogs med bzang po). *Byang chub sems dpa'i spyod pa la 'jug pa'i 'grel pa legs par bshad pa'i rgya mtsho*. Sarnath, India: Pleasure of Elegant Sayings Printing Press, 1974.

Medicine
[W H I T E]
(Chapters 4, 6, 9, 15, 19, 23, 26, 31)

Badiner, Allan, and Alex Grey, eds. *Zig Zag Zen: Buddhism and Psychedelics*. 2002; Santa Fe: Synergetic, 2015.

Burroughs, William S., and Allen Ginsberg. *The Yage Letters: Redux*. Ed. Oliver Harris. New York: Penguin, 2008.

Castaneda, Carlos. *Journey to Ixtlan*. New York: Simon and Schuster, 1972.

Demange, François. *Metsa: De l'ombre à la lumière: Voyages d'un guérisseur chez les chamanes*. Paris: Mama, 2014.

Guerra, Ciro. *Embrace of the Serpent (El abrazo de la serpiente)*. Feature film, 2015.

Hari, Johann. *Chasing the Scream: The First and Last Days of the War on Drugs*. London: Bloomsbury, 2015.

Huxley, Aldous. *The Doors of Perception* and *Heaven and Hell*. New York: Harper and Row, 1963. *Doors of Perception* first published in 1954.

———. *The Perennial Philosophy*. London: Chatto and Windus, 1946.

Levinas, Emmanuel. *Ethics and Infinity: Conversations with Philippe Nemo*. Trans. Richard A. Cohen. Pittsburgh: Duquesne University Press, 1985.

McKenna, Terence. *Food of the Gods: The Search for the Original Tree of Knowledge*. New York: Bantam, 1992.

Osto, Douglas. *Altered States: Buddhism and Psychedelic Spirituality in America*. New York: Columbia University Press, 2016.

Pinchbeck, Daniel. *Breaking Open the Head: A Psychedelic Journey into the Heart of Contemporary Shamanism*. New York: Broadway, 2002.

Pollan, Michael. *How to Change Your Mind: The New Science of Psychedelics*. New York: Penguin, 2018.

Wilson, Frances. *Guilty Thing: A Life of Thomas De Quincey*. London: Bloomsbury, 2016.

[Tobacco statistics: https://www.cdc.gov/tobacco/data_statistics/ fact_sheets/fast_facts/index.htm; alcohol statistics: https://www .niaaa.nih.gov/alcohol-health/overview-alcohol-consumption/ alcohol-facts-and-statistics.]

Philosophy

[BLUE]

(Chapters 2, 5, 10, 13, 18, 24, 27, 29)

Bakewell, Sarah. *How to Live: A Life of Montaigne in One Question and Twenty Attempts at an Answer*. London: Vintage, 2010.

Carlisle, Claire. *Philosopher of the Heart: The Restless Life of Søren Kierkegaard*. London: Allen Lane, 2019.

Conche, Marcel. *Pyrrhon ou l'apparence*. Paris: PUF, 1994.

Desan, Philippe. *Montaigne: A Life*. Trans. Steven Rendall and Lisa Neal. Princeton: Princeton University Press, 2017. (*Montaigne: Une biographie politique*. Paris: Odile Jacob, 2014.)

Ellis, Robert M. *The Buddha's Middle Way: Experiential Judgment in His Life and Teaching*. Sheffield: Equinox, 2019.

Emerson, Ralph Waldo. *Representative Men: Seven Lectures*. Boston: Phillips, Sampson, 1850.

Greenblatt, Stephen. *The Rise and Fall of Adam and Eve*. London: Vintage, 2017.

———. *The Swerve: How the World Became Modern*. New York: Norton, 2011.

Greenblatt, Stephen, and Peter G. Platt, eds. *Shakespeare's Montaigne: The Florio Translation of the Essays*. New York: New York Review Books, 2014.

Lenoir, Frédéric. *Le miracle Spinoza: Une philosophie pour éclairer notre vie*. Paris: Fayard, 2017.

Lucretius. *The Nature of Things*. Trans. A. E. Stallings. London: Penguin, 2007.

Montaigne, Michel de. *Montaigne: Les Essais*. Adapted into modern French by André Lanly. Paris: Gallimard, 2009.

————. *The Complete Essays.* Trans. and ed. M. A. Screech. London: Penguin, 1991.

————. *Les Essais: Édition conforme au texte de l'exemplaire de Bordeaux.* Ed. Pierre Villey. Paris: PUF, 1924.

Vázquez, Manuel Bermúdez. *Philosophical Scepticism and Its Tradition in Michel de Montaigne's Essais.* Ph.D. thesis, University of Edinburgh, 2012.

Appendix

Norman, K. R., trans. *The Group of Discourses* (Sutta Nipāta). Oxford: Pali Text Society, 2001.

acknowledgments

I am indebted to the Daughters of Fortune—Léa Fages, Monique Bisson, Martine Batchelor, Evelyne Fages-Decortes, Léna Decortes, Judith Bisson, Constance Bisson, Valentine Bisson, and Cécile Bisson—for the crucial role they played in the organization of the material.

I am deeply grateful to my agent Anne Edelstein and editor Jennifer Banks for their dedication and care in bringing *The Art of Solitude* into the world. I also thank Cindy Spiegel for her insightful editorial input and unwavering enthusiasm for the project.

My understanding of the political context of Montaigne's life is drawn primarily from Philippe Desan's magisterial *Montaigne: Une biographie politique* (English: *Montaigne: A Life*).

Throughout the writing of this book, I have been inspired, supported, kept in check, and challenged by my colleagues and students at Bodhi College. Thank you all.

I wish to acknowledge the influence of the writings of William S. Burroughs, Ernest Hemingway, Karl Ove Knausgaard, and Georges Perec on this book.

Numerous other individuals have contributed to *The Art of Solitude,* whether they were aware of it or not. In particular, I would like to thank Keren Arbel, Yelena Avramenko, Allan Badiner, David Batchelor, Charlie Blacklock, Susan Blackmore, André van der Braak, Leigh Brasington, Guy Claxton, Régine Coleman, Anne Marie de Winter, Robert Ellis, Christina Feldman, Danielle Follett, Gil Fronsdal, Sarah Gillespie, Richard Gombrich, Antony Gormley, Manon Grier, Joan Halifax, Dan Heaton, Winton Higgins, Nancy Holt, Hyonho Sunim, Dora Kalff, Elisabeth Kools, Robert Kull, Stefan Lang, Christian Mähler-Besse, Nacho Maldondo Martínez, Ramsey Margolis, Ken McLeod, Thomas Metzinger, Vanja Palmers, John Peacock, Julie Püttgen, Stephen Schettini, Rainer Scheurenbrand, Renate Seifarth, Shantum Seth, Carmel Shalev, Andrés Sierra, Jason Siff, Carina Stone, Tom Tillemans, Don Toño, Helen Tworkov, Manuel Villaescusa, Gay Watson, Akincano Weber, Jenny Wilks, and Sean Williams.

index